CONCILIUM

CONCILIUM   2008/3

JESUS AS CHRIST: WHAT IS AT STAKE IN CHRISTOLOGY?

Edited by
Andrés Torres Queiruga, Lisa Sowle Cahill,
Maria Clara Bingemer and Erik Borgman

SCM Press · London

Published by SCM Press, 13–17 Long Lane, London EC1A 9PN

Copyright © International Association of Conciliar Theology, Madras (India)

English translations copyright © 2008 SCM-Canterbury Press Ltd

ISBN 978 0 334 03099 7

Printed in the UK by
CPI William Clowes Beccles NR34 7TL

Concilium published March, June, August, October,
December

Contents

II. Documentation/Theological Forum

Editorial
What is at Stake in Christology

Christology is still the nerve centre in which all the cross-currents of Christian understanding and theological reflection make themselves felt. It is the crossroads at which decisive questions meet and where the basic contents of the faith are put to the test, both inwardly toward the church community and outwardly toward relationships with culture.

In this sense, it might well be said that christology is going through a sort of 'second modernity'. The first came into being when biblical criticism forced the interpretation of the mystery of Christ through concepts inherited from the Fathers and the Scholastics to be revised, imposing abandonment of the – till then normal – literalist reading of the texts. The beginnings of the second can – for Catholicism, not without the fraternal influence of Protestant theology – be assigned to Vatican II, when not only was the need to continue what had been started recognized, but its cultivation received an official boost. In this process, the shift from the twentieth to the twenty-first century has brought about a lively re-assessment of the christological tradition, thanks mainly to, on the one hand, the new socio-cultural contextualization of Jesus and his Good News (well represented by the 'Third Quest'), and, on the other, to influential impacts springing from the new culture: the dialogue among religions, the practical impulses provided by liberation theologies, the theoretical broadening provided by the cultural horizons of Asia and Africa, and finally the deeper analysis of what is human brought about by feminist thinking.

All of this has produced a most lively resurgence of the decisive question: 'Who do "they" say, and who do "you" say that I am?' And once again the linkage of the two poles of the christological mystery face theology with the challenge of finding a balance that will do justice both to the specific humanity of Jesus and to the mystery we seek to express by talking of his divinity. Without preservation of the divine aspect the innermost essence of Christian

7

identity would be lost; without the realism of his humanity the possibility of following him would be annulled and his saving efficacy blurred: *quod super nos, nihil ad nos.* The balance is not easy and requires equal measures of respect for our heritage and freedom to convert it into living proclamation in the changing settings of historical embodiment in the social and cultural contexts of our age.

It all makes us think that the deepest movement is leading to a new understanding of the humanity of Jesus, the Christ. Centuries of christology marked by the lofty reflection of the fourth Gospel and by the dogmatic pronouncement of Chalcedon changed the divinity of Christ into such a dominant starting point that it is appropriate to speak of a sort of a-historical 'Monophytism' in theological speculation and of a certain 'mythologism' in popular imagery. Today it no longer possible to continue with a vision that, as has so often been said, tends to regard Jesus as a divine being who descended from on high and passed through our world only to return to heaven. There is a real hunger for rescuing the reality of his human life, of his fellowship in the flesh with our sorrows and joys, with our quests and our hopes – in a word, of being able to see him and feel him as a model for our lives who, secure in the love of God, gave himself up to effective love of his brothers and sisters and opened himself out to the great hope of the final Kingdom.

In fact, this widespread perception by our cultural sensitivities is convergent with the results, which we see as firm and irreversible, of critical studies of the New Testament. These have broken the monopoly of a forcedly unified view of Jesus the Christ, discounting the multiple and many-sided wealth present in the various writings. An interpretation that is open and faithful to all his teachings is not in any way opposed to the confession of faith but rather shows it truly *incarnate* in a Jesus who, in his relationship to his *Abba* and in his self-bestowal on his brothers and sisters, appears 'like us in all things but sin' (Heb. 4.15). To ignore the variety of this wealth, reducing it to a single viewpoint, however lofty or sublime it might appear, far from shedding light on profession of faith, runs the risk of de-incarnating Christ, clothing him in our human – perhaps all too human – projections, instead of 'learning him' humbly in the lowliness and reality of his flesh.

There have been and still are abuses, and theology needs to be constantly alert to any reductionism that proves blind to the inexhaustible depth of the christological mystery. But it would not be good, for example, for distaste for and even protest against the unworthiness and dishonesty of some pseudo-historical publications to lead us to deny the legitimacy of the movement as a whole and even to ignore the fact that the deformations themselves contain the proclamation of a real longing for *human* communion with God. And of course there is absolutely no need for full recognition of his humanity to paralyze theological reflection, preventing the confession of faith, which is not limited to seeing in Jesus only 'the carpenter's son' (Matt. 13.55) but which also guides us critically toward the confession that 'truly this man was God's Son' (Mark 15.39). Accepting Jesus' humanity in all its admirable integrity can and should today be perhaps the best way of confessing his divinity as the Christ, in that mysterious dialectic that marks the unique specificity of his person and which, though without exclusivisms of any kind, grounds the full and definitive character of his Good News.

Concilium, started to contribute to the fulfilment and ongoing development of Vatican II's solemn undertaking, can naturally not stand aside from this concern. The long-pondered decision to devote an issue to these questions was encouraged and confirmed by the publication of *Jesus of Nazareth*, signed – in a gesture that appears to be unique in history – by Joseph Ratzinger/Benedict XVI. We recognize the importance of his decision, obviously intended to insist firmly on the essential values of a 'high' christology of Johannine stamp and thereby to confirm confession of the divinity of Christ for Christian consciousness and to the benefit of the world. This is a proper duty of a pastor who is concerned above all with upholding the continuity of tradition. His voice should be heard.

But, as he himself states in proclaiming the freedom that should go with reading his book ('Everyone has the liberty to contradict me'; p. 20), theology cannot abandon the other pole. Welcoming the original mandate to 'make your defence to anyone who demands from you an account of the hope that is in you' (1 Pet. 3.15), it also has a mission to show that fidelity is demonstrated not only by upholding continuity across cultural changes but also by taking creative advantage of the new things these changes usher in and responding to the questions and needs that gave rise to them. At a time of radical change such as our own, the latter becomes one of the most vital tasks for theology, if it is the case that its particular concern is the effort to make the word of God a living word, capable of giving life through its meaningfulness to each and every moment of history.

This issue of *Concilium*, conscious of the huge task today facing the entire theological community, seeks to join in with the many efforts now being made. It does not claim to offer a systematic treatment. As its very structure shows, it seeks only to shed light on some major points.

The articles in the first part, questing for a truly incarnate christology, bear on three main fronts: (1) current re-reading of the biblical texts concerning Jesus, in their hermeneutical multiplicity (Roger Haight) and their rootedness in the tradition and history of his people (Sean Freyne); (2) the basic problem of Jesus' complete humanity, which makes him open to the divine (Andrés Torres Queiruga), in the sense that he transcends any discrimination based on the difference between men and women (Maria Clara Bingemer), and that he opens up a universal salvation through his loving self-sacrifice on the cross, free of any juridical grievance (Lisa Sowle Cahill); (3) the coming about of God's saving presence in the proclamation and fulfilment of the Kingdom (Jon Sobrino), in the bodily specificity of all human history (Erik Borgman), and in fraternal encounter with other cultures and religions (Felix Wilfred).

The subjects in the documentation section correspond to two main concerns: (1) the varied reception of the figure of Jesus: an overview of images of him in contemporary theology (Robert Schreiter), a panorama of the reception of Ratzinger/Benedict XVI's book on Jesus (Rosino Gibellini), and a summary account of some publications on research into the historical Jesus (José Antonio Pagola); (2) concern over a certain authoritarianism on the part of the magisterium in both doctrinal, particularly christological, matters (José Ignacio González Faus) and in more directly socio-cultural affairs (Karl Gabriel), in liturgical prayer itself (Hanspeter Heinz), and, finally, as an attempt to rein back the dynamism of the council on such a sensitive and vital subject as revelation (Silvia Scatena)

Maria Clara Bingemer, Erik Borgman, Lisa Sowle Cahill,
Andrés Torres Queiruga

I. Jesus as Christ

Scripture: A Pluralistic Norm for Understanding our Salvation in Jesus Christ

ROGER HAIGHT

Introduction

The phrase 'pluralistic norm' accurately describes the New Testament as a collection of writings and how it functions in the church. But the phrase also contains a paradox: it is difficult to conceive how a norm can be pluralistic, or how a pluralistic document can be normative. It does not resolve issues; it leaves them open. This essay will discuss this apparent dilemma and try to show why and how the pluralistic character of our scripture proves to be its consistent strength. While what is said here applies to the Bible as a whole, I will focus my attention on the New Testament because the more focused subject matter alluded to is our understanding of Jesus Christ.

There is much to be said on this very expansive topic, and to treat it in a short space requires a thin line-sketch in lieu of a portrait. But from another perspective, many of the problems connected with this subject matter are products of uncritical conceptions naively learned. To meet this prior problem head-on I shall try to build these reflections from below. I begin with a simple account of some background notions, definitions, and descriptions of basic ideas. I shall then trace how we can conceive this issue generatively: that is, by following the story of the emergence of the New Testament and describing how it functions empirically and theologically in the community. I shall do this in five steps with considerations of how we know transcendent reality, scripture as a continuing mediation of God to our consciousness, the idea of a pluralistic norm, how it represents experiences of salvation, and various conceptions of the person of Jesus Christ.

I. Mediation, sacramentalism, symbolism, iconic mystagogy

The question of religious knowledge, how human beings are able to know transcendent reality and speak about it with any realism, is a serious and delicate problem that will never cease to be debated. Very few, if any, meaningful suppositions are universally agreed upon. But I shall work with one that has wide acceptance: all our contact with transcendent reality is mediated. By mediation I mean that transcendent reality, the sphere of God that transcends finite reality and knowledge, cannot enter our consciousness directly but always and only through the finite world of which we are a part.

One way to explain this idea of mediation lies in distinguishing dimensions of the human relationship to transcendent reality. God is directly or immediately present to the human subject; this is entailed in the conception of creation out of nothing, where nothing lies between the creature and God.[1] But while God is immediately present to us, we cannot be immediately present to God in our consciousness but can only respond consciously through mediation. I am not aware of any possibility of escaping that premise without somehow escaping our bodies. As long as we are bodies, our consciousness, even our deepest self-consciousness where we are beings-present-to-ourselves, is a mediated consciousness. This spiritual being-present-to-ourselves cannot not be mediated through our specific, bodily, and sensible selves. This being tied to matter is the ultimate basis of individuality, historical consciousness, pluralism, and our inability to encounter God directly or immediately.[2] After Marx's and Mannheim's sociology of knowledge and Freud's critique of the subconscious, it is difficult to see how direct encounter with God could be conceived. The Bible portrays God interacting with humans through media or emissaries. Not even the mystic's encounter with God is immediate. The deepest or the most ecstatic states of consciousness represent a 'there where' the self is most intensely, reflectively, and transparently gathered into itself, providing the aperture where God's presence is mediated and hence experienced. The accounts of great theologians, such as Schleiermacher's and Rahner's phenomenology, Augustine's Neo-platonic ascent, and Aquinas' and Blondel's analyses of the dynamics of intellect and will respectively, more deeply portray this mediation than do the shortcuts of 'immediate encounter.'

The insistence on *sensible* mediation has two functions, one negative and the other positive. On the negative side, it keeps the theological imagination tied to history. The insistence contains an implicit critique of theology that begins too far above the ground and drifts ever higher without looking down to where people actually are. The positive side is that the imagination, tied to sensible data, is precisely the platform for the sacramental or so-called Catholic imagination. The discussion of the role of the imagination and sacramentality represents this dynamic, mystagogical, creative, and constructive role of imagination.[3] It is, of course, absolutely important not to underplay the presence and power of God immediately at work in the human subject. The *tabula* is less *rasa* than Aristotle or Aquinas thought. Mediation, however, does not subtract from divine presence, but is fed by God as Spirit or cooperative grace.

Christian theology has a variety of ideas and phrases that in slightly different accents refer to this common language of mediation. A 'sacramental imagination' is one that can read the spiritual in the material, because the whole world is the creator's sacrament. The 'sacrament's' outward, tangible, or physical face mediates the inward, spiritual, and divine action. The 'symbol,' in particular the religious symbol, is sacramental: the symbol represents and makes present what is other than itself. The 'icon' functions analogously to a symbol or a sacrament. And the response to an icon is 'mystagogical.' People with spiritual sensibility resonate with the dynamics of mystagogy: the religious symbol or icon draws human consciousness into itself and directs it in an ascending direction to 'participate' in transcendent reality. In sum, all of these rather basic ideas are the subjects of technical debate and a large variety of nuanced interpretations. But they also correspond with and elicit ordinary and extraordinary religious experiences which religious people in some measure share.

II. Scripture (New Testament) as norm

The nature of scripture, the various qualities it shares in Christian doctrine such as its inspiration and inerrancy, its place in the Christian community as the common, shared historical authority, and how it actually plays that role in the community at large and among the ranks of its theologians all merit careful consideration. These fundamental issues include different conceptions of particular everyday problems, and one cannot avoid taking some positions in this area. I hope that I can state some widely accepted principles that, despite their broad generic character, will also have some bearing on the topic. Three conceptions seem important: a description of the status of scripture, the dogmatic appreciation of it, and its necessity for the Christian community.

First, from a historical perspective, scripture is accurately described as a record of the religious experience of the Jewish and then the Christian community. The scriptures did not fall from heaven; they were written by authors, put together by editors or collectors, in communities, whose perspective they reflect. The critical approach to scripture in the modern period has greatly enhanced the realism with which we now think about the formation of the scriptures. Learning the story of the coming to be of each scriptural writing, to the extent that it can be reconstructed, deepens appreciation of its distinctiveness. The wide variety of literary genres in the Bible cannot fail to impress the seeker of religious truth.

Second, however, Christians are not alone in thinking that their scriptures are inspired and inerrant. What can these doctrines mean in an age of biblical criticism? They need not negate the empirical historical facts of human authors; but they do affirm the role of a transcendent presence and divine guidance in the process. They need not be conceived exclusively with reference to individual authors, or naively imagined as a whispering in the ear; they could simply refer to the faith conviction of God's presence to whatever historical events provoked their composition. Whether or not any particular author or editor was 'inspired,' the New Testament communities bear strong witness to the presence of the Spirit of God at work in their midst. Faith is assured of this sacred character of the scriptures: they draw human consciousness into God's sphere.

Third, these interpretations of the doctrines support the necessity of the scriptures and their enthroned position in the community. That necessity finds its logic in the linear character of history and the inexorable fact that things change, memory fades, and without a record Christian origins will lose their hold on the consciousness of the community. If Jewish and Christian faith alike have historical moorings, a firm corporate conviction that certain events of history have constituted the very existence of each and given it a certain character, and that God was present in these events, then memory of them constitutes these communities and forgetfulness means dissolution. If something real about God was revealed in Moses and Jesus, loss of memory would be loss in that particular relationship. Being bound to our past by these classic preservations of it involves the identity of these religious communities. They are necessary for their existence. They are the norms of their identities.

III. A Pluralistic Norm

This leads to the heart of the problem: what is a pluralistic norm? Does the paradox in the phrase imply internal contradiction? Let me propose a way of understanding a 'pluralistic norm' in order to see whether it fits what we know of the formation of the New Testament and the way it functions in the Christian community.

It seems clear that, in the case of science and mathematical calculation, one cannot operate in a framework that allows plural systems and criteria for evidence. There are human communities that can only work on a command-obey system of normativity. The regimentation of some spheres of human life, such as the military or bureaucracies, cannot work with the efficiency they are designed to provide when a plurality of norms are simultaneously dictating behaviour. But religious authority is *sui generis* because knowledge of the transcendent religious object which commands authority is not directly available. Religious authority is only truly religious insofar as its authority comes from a genuinely transcendent source. And because that object is not immediately accessible, but only available through its finite, particular, and historically conditioned media, human beings have to be content with interpretations of different stripes. In the end, the natural condition of human existence itself is pluralistic, so that all communitarian religious commitment is pluralistic whether it be across religions traditions or within any single religious community. On the one hand, no religious authority can escape our finite historical condition; on the other, all religious communities should expect other valid mediations of the 'same' transcendent reality.

Does this view, based as it is on a historically-conscious epistemological account of religious experience, correspond with what we know of the formation of the New Testament? Those who have studied the New Testament are aware that the writings that make up this book were written along the way over an extended period of time. Some of the letters attributed to Paul are authentic and make up the first, oldest, and most historically authentic texts of the New Testament. The gospel accounts of Luke and Matthew were cobbled together from Mark, another common source, and other private sources; most if not all of the material was created and first preserved in oral form. John's Gospel seems to have been written after the other Gospels and is a quite distinctive product of a particular community. We do not know the actual authors of other texts beyond Paul, or those who collected the material into various other writings; the best that can be said of many of the letters of the New Testament is that they were the products of certain communities and perhaps intended to be read widely by others. Both factors help to explain their distinctiveness. This description of the formation of the writings contained in the New Testament correlates nicely with the idea of the generation of a pluralistic norm.

There is more to be said about the nature of a pluralistic norm. But before moving to that discussion it may be helpful simply to indicate without development some of the pointed advantages that such a norm preserves. The balance of 'multiple norms' within the New Testament package prevents the absolutization of any single norm. One book of the New Testament does not trump another, nor one metaphor another. At the same time, the New Testament as a collection of witnesses can clearly exclude many interpretations or judgments as un-Christian. Time and again in the course of human history the New Testament has been brought to bear as a final negative norm. Moreover, it seems inevitable that the New Testament as a whole imposes authoritatively on the Christian community itself an openness to pluralism. Insofar as the universal Christian community accepts the New Testament as the most basic norm of itself, in the same measure the pluralistic character of the New Testament authoritatively imposes on that community its own pluralism. It will become apparent in the next section that this is not a failure or deficiency of the New Testament, but precisely a compelling invitation to become a creative, interpreting, and inculturating community in history.

IV. Salvation as Union with God and Fellow Human Beings

The discussion up to this point has avoided a clear delineation of the meaning of pluralism. Such a definition has direct bearing on the questions of soteriology and christology to which I now turn.

The idea of pluralism that controls this discussion means 'unity amid diversity.' From the opposite perspective one can look upon pluralism as differences that obtain within a larger field or sphere of unity. It is important to distinguish this pluralism from sheer diversity or plurality. A deep analogy of partial difference and partial sameness holds a plurality of members together within a set. With this understanding of pluralism, we are in a position to understand the notion of 'salvation' pluralistically.

What is 'salvation'? Any short response to this question will fail to do justice to this religious category. The intention guiding this development goes no further than pointing to the external framework within which one may begin to think about this profound issue. As a point of departure for such an indication few things are more important than recognizing that the question of salvation is a fundamentally human question, essentially universal because inescapable, which arises existentially as an intrinsic dimension in a self-conscious, reflective, free, decisive, and hence spiritual human existence. The spirituality and the freedom of the human being are virtually identical, and together they release the question of self-identity, of where the human person as such comes from, and most pressingly where it is going. These issues constitute the religious question because they elicit or demand ultimate answers of a negative or a positive kind. In either case, what is at stake is the meaningfulness of human existence, where meaning itself, let alone its comprehensiveness, is as far as we know a distinguishing mark of the human. Salvation, at its root, refers to a positive response to the religious question. To experience salvation is to encounter that which gives meaning and a positive destiny to human existence.

Christians experience salvation as coming from God and as mediated by Jesus Christ. In the remaining portion of this section I will simply state what all Christians know: that Jesus is saviour from God, that that salvation may be expressed in a variety of ways, but that all those expressions of salvation point to one generically or abstractly stated salvation that is one and the same for all.

Each book in the New Testament in its own way testifies to Jesus of Nazareth as one sent by God for human salvation, or at least is based on that premise and draws out it consequences. That Jesus is saviour is the Christian answer to the religious question, and the foundational experience that constitutes at its core Christian faith in God. Jesus of Nazareth is the fundamental Christian mediation of God, the central concrete symbol, sacrament, and icon through which Christians encounter the transcendent reality of God.

The more specific meaning of this salvation, the way in which Jesus mediated it, and the way in which it is appropriated are expressed in several different ways. During the 1970s Edward Schillebeeckx wrote an exhaustive study of how New Testament authors construed the salvation mediated by Jesus through an extensive analysis of each book of the New Testament.[4] He found a great variety in the ways in which the New Testament expressed what the salvation mediated by Jesus was like: a new creation, an adoption by

God, so that one becomes a child of God, or one receives the Holy Spirit of God; one becomes freed from one's sin; one is redeemed, bought and paid for, reconciled with God, and with other human beings; Jesus renders satisfaction for our sin, functions as a sin-offering, mediates the forgiveness of our sins, justifies us, sanctifies us, represents us before God; through Jesus we are freed, from our sin, from our debts, for life in the community, for the love of others, for commitment to God, into life in full flourishing, and a renewal of the earth. One never has a sense of having to choose which one of these images is the right one: they are all right, and yet they are really quite different conceptions.

But despite this extravagant plurality and diversity of conception, one can formulate an understanding, abstract relative to the elaboration of each one of these images, yet realistically descriptive of a common experience and response of all Christians. All Christians encountered God as saviour in Jesus of Nazareth, God coming close in and through him so that he mediates to them, to their consciousness and to their persons, a way of responding and relating to God. The question of salvation allows one to recognize with great clarity how the New Testament offers a pluralistic norm for understanding Christian salvation. Salvation in the end is union with God and union with one's fellow human beings in a way that guarantees one's identity and destiny. But that can be understood concretely in a variety of different ways.

V. Christologies

Just as the New Testament contains a pluralism of soteriologies, so too one finds a multiplicity of different christologies in its pages. By christology I means the interpretation and understanding of who Jesus of Nazareth was and is. Obviously people had various appreciations of his identity during his ministry, but these are quite difficult, if not impossible, to reconstruct. In any case, interpretation of his identity took on a qualitatively different character in the light of the experience that Jesus was risen and the framework this supplied.

The relation between soteriology and christology, or more concretely expressed, between the experience of salvation mediated through Jesus and the interpretation of his personal identity, provides a crucial key to christological interpretation generally. A historically-conscious christology studies the development of the interpretation of Jesus as Lord, as best the sources will allow. I shall not trace various reconstructions of that development but only note how the communities' experiences of salvation provided grounds for various christological interpretations. It was not the case that people regarded Jesus as a messenger, a kind of mailman, who delivered a message from God. A much closer analogy and thus a better symbol would liken him to the ambassador who was fully authorized to be the message: the message and its content were tied up in his embodying them. The one who bore salvation from God participated in the divine agency. We thus find a certain correlation between conceptions of how Jesus mediated salvation and his identity as the one who mediated it to the disciples. The ensuing development included an increasing appreciation that this salvation was universally relevant, a reality for all humankind, the destiny of human existence itself.

It is difficult to count exactly how many different christologies one could find in the New Testament; different exegetes would come up with different results according to the breadth of their criteria for what constituted a discernable and distinct conception. In *Jesus Symbol of God*, without any intention of being exhaustive, I raised up five christologies as examples that are quite distinct from each other. These were named 'Jesus Christ as the Last Adam' in the Pauline writings, 'Jesus Christ as Son of God' in Mark, 'Jesus Christ as empowered by the Spirit of God' in Luke, 'Jesus Christ as Wisdom of God', which can be found in the Pauline tradition and also in Matthew's Gospel, and finally 'Jesus Christ as the Word of God' as that is especially rendered in John's Prologue.[5] There is considerable diversity among these christologies and a wide range of interpreting both what they meant in their context and how they can be appropriated today. Not all of these christologies stress Jesus' personal divinity, and those that appear to are not always clear about what 'divinity' means. A christology that seemed to imply a supernatural provenance of Jesus by referring to him as 'the Son of Man' did not progress very far in the tradition. And the designation that Jesus was Son of God, which originally had no connotation of a divine figure in any realistic sense, developed ultimately into a quite literal title. Thus the development of christology in the period of the composition of the New Testament writings was considerable and did not cease afterwards. Judging from writing in the area, it has not ceased today either.

Can one understand this plurality of christologies as constituting a pluralism, that is, cohering in a common field that binds them together? The ability to do this would provide a key for how christological discussion could be open and critical on a deep theological level yet not divisive of the community. The answer to this question cannot be given in terms of one absolute christology that imposes itself at the expense of the others. The nature of the problem itself forbids such a solution because of the inability of historically-conditioned and limited statements to encompass all points of view. Rather the solution has to lie in the distinction between faith and statements of theology and belief. Such a faith can be described: it is the intelligent commitment to Jesus as the Christ and the one who mediates God's salvation to human beings. A theology of Jesus Christ that coherently accounts for that commitment is by the criteria of the discipline adequate or orthodox. If it accounts for the data of scripture, is intelligible in terms of a contemporary understanding of reality, and empowers Christian life after the pattern of Jesus' own preaching, it is an orthodox christology. That there can be several irreducible christologies that fill those criteria is proved by the New Testament itself.

Conclusion

Gerd Theissen writes that the 'canon is the great achievement of early catholic primitive Christianity. . . . It is decisive that the canon did not suppress the inner plurality of primitive Christianity, but preserved it.'[6] Part of the problem we have in accepting the pluralism of scripture lies with a history of interpretation that has projected back into its pages later interpretations that gradually became taken for granted. It is actually quite difficult not to find one's own standard views reinforced by scriptural texts. Biblical criticism did much to correct this problem, but the lack of communication between exegetes and theologians remains. Mixed up with this are conceptions of religious epistemology, revelation, and faith that do not quite allow the transcendent mystery of God its due. The absolute importance of religious truth obscures the degree to which all conceptions of it are historically conditioned and thus limited. Without a certain amount of humility and openness to other possibilities of genuine revelation of transcendent truth, the religious sensibility becomes perverted in a competitive framework of understanding the relation of the religions to each other. Instead of conversation and mutual learning between the religions, debate turns into competition, then hostility, and sometimes violence. In this way the reduction of transcendent truth to our formulas about it translates religious pluralism into religious antagonism, and divine revelation is simply negated in the reduction of religion to power and pragmatic control. The pluralism of the New Testament actually teaches and prescribes for Christian consciousness a completely different attitude toward divine authority, one which precisely protects human freedom by eliciting a response to its universal appeal by a commitment to love and reconciliation with a generous God who shows no partiality.

Notes

1. One can add layers to this immediacy, as does Rahner with his idea of God's personal self-communication distinct from creative personal presence. And this makes a difference ontologically: surely the being of humans is different under the influence of God's love and gift of self than it would be without these.

2. Psychologically these experiences will have a note of 'immediacy', and hence the language of 'mediated immediacy' has descriptive relevance; it is a postulate or theory or theological construction that fits the data. But more deeply or ontologically, the 'immediacy' applies to God, the 'mediated' describes human appropriation of God.

3. I discuss the role of the imagination in religious knowledge and christology in Roger Haight, *The Future of Christology*, New York: Continuum, 2005, pp. 13–31.

4. Edward Schillebeeckx, *Christ: The Experience of Jesus as Lord*, New York: Seabury Press, 1980. Schillebeeckx covered all the New Testament writings other than the Synoptic Gospels, which he had considered earlier in *Jesus: An Experiment in Christology*, New York: Seabury Press, 1979.

5. Roger Haight, *Jesus Symbol of God*, Maryknoll, NY: Orbis Books, 1999, pp. 155–78.

6. *Ibid.*

Jesus the Jew

SEAN FREYNE

In a recent book entitled *The Misunderstood Jew. The Church and the Scandal of the Jewish Jesus* (2006), the New Testament scholar Ami-Jill Levine, herself Jewish, trenchantly berates Christian preachers and teachers for the often blatant anti-Jewish tendencies in their statements and writings. Even liberal Christian New Testament scholarship that prides itself on objective and critical approaches does not escape her witty but incisive exposure of the deeply engrained habits of a super-sessionist theology. There can be no denying that many of the more obvious examples of Christian anti-Judaism are already inscribed in Christian canonical texts. They therefore require a critical and self-critical hermeneutic on both the historical and theological levels. The caricature of the Pharisees, the blaming of Jews for the death of Jesus and the exoneration of the Romans, the alleged superficiality of Jewish piety in contrast to Jesus' pure religion from the heart, these and many other topics are familiar discussion points for anybody engaged in contemporary Jewish and Christian dialogue. Indeed, in my experience, it is only when one comes face to face with people whose practice of their Jewish faith is both living and vibrant that one comes to realize just how distorted many of Christianity's inherited and unquestioned stereotypes of Jews and Judaism really are.

The question of Jesus' Jewish faith and piety has inevitably come under particular scrutiny in the light of current interest in the historical Jesus. Levine reports that from her critical perspective 'the historical Jesus is not good news for Jews.' Sadly, even a passing perusal of some of the recent construals suggests that her judgment is all too true. The Galilean Jesus, the Mediterranean Jesus, the Cynic Jesus, the Jesus who abandons purity concerns for mercy and love, the feminist Jesus – these and other claims about Jesus are often built on portrayals of Judaism that are ill-founded, offensive, and highly selective.

The recent book by the current Pope, Benedict XVI, alias Joseph

Ratzinger, *Jesus of Nazareth* (English translation, 2007), is a classic case in point. There can be no doubting the author's desire to be respectful to Jewish sensitivities, and to this end he engages in dialogue with the Jewish author Rabbi Jacob Neusner, who had previously published a book entitled *A Rabbi talks with Jesus* (2000). The Pope also wishes to correct the false impression created by Christian scholars about Jesus, which, in his opinion, has led to a confusion among Catholic Christians and a weakening of faith in Jesus as the sole and unique saviour. However, in his desire to reaffirm the uniqueness of Jesus for Christian faith he falls into the trap of presenting Jesus' ministry and teaching as transcending the bounds of his own faith and culture. Thus, to cite one of many possible examples, he writes: 'From this vantage point (i.e. Jesus' eschatological awareness) we can see clearly that Jesus is a "true Israelite" (cf. John 1.47) and also that – in terms of the inner dynamics of the promises made to Israel – *he transcends Judaism*' (p. 57, italics added). This idea of transcending Judaism has its pay-off a little later when Ratzinger presents us with the typical stereotype of the Pharisees. 'There are two ways to God and to self,' we are told. 'The Pharisee does not look at God at all, but only at himself; he does not really need God, because he does everything right by himself. He has no real relationship with God, who is ultimately superfluous – what he does himself is enough' (p. 62).

I do not wish to labour the point or enter into a full discussion of the Pope's book here. However, the examples just given demonstrate how easy it is to 'vilify the other in order to define the self,' thereby creating dualisms that are blinkered, damaging, and erroneous. The two contrasting attitudes that the Pope wishes to present – being totally dependent on God, or being self-sufficient and smug – are not by any means the prerogative of first-century Jews! The analysis of 'the Pharisee and the Publican' story fails to note that this is a parable, which often exaggerates for the effect it seeks to bring about in the hearer/reader, and further that this story is only found in the Gospel of Luke, who was writing at a point in time when Jewish-Christian relations were far removed from the situation in Jesus' day. Caricature and vilification were often the order of the day in the literature on both sides of the growing divide between the parent and the sibling. But even if we leave aside historical criticism (which elsewhere in the book the Pope vigorously defends), one is tempted to ask: What was the Pharisee doing in the temple anyhow, if 'he did not need God'?!

In the remainder of this essay I will address briefly the historical and theological issues that arise when one enquires about the Jewish Jesus.

I. Historical Considerations

To begin with it is important to have a clear picture of how the terms 'Jew' and 'Jewish' are being used in the discussion. Too often they are used as generalized descriptions of the other, as we have just seen, ignoring completely the fact that, then as now, Jewish faith and practice had taken on a number of different, even competing forms. Very often the four philosophies of which the Jewish historian Josephus speaks (Pharisees, Sadducees, Essenes and Zealots) are used as shorthand for the totality of first-century Judaism. If any attention is given to others outside these groups, it is usually the Jews of the Diaspora that are meant, or, occasionally, the great unwashed 'people of the land' (the *'am ha-aretz* of some later texts), who were deemed to be ignorant of even the basics of Jewish observance.

Some time ago E. P. Sanders sought to correct this picture by speaking of a common Judaism, which consists of a set of practices and beliefs that were shared by all who thought of themselves as *Ioudaioi*. It should be recalled that Judaism, unlike Christianity, did not have an extended set of beliefs set out in credal form and enjoined by some central authority. Orthopraxis, rather than orthodoxy, was the chief concern, in terms of the defining realities. These consisted of belief in one God, creator and saviour of Israel, whose will was revealed to Moses in the Torah. This God was to be worshipped through observance of the Sabbath and other stipulations of the Decalogue. Attendance at the temple for the great festivals was expected, and this involved the bringing of agricultural and other offerings for the priests. Circumcision of new-born males was seen as an initiation rite into the community of Israel, and belief in the future redemption of Israel was variously understood. Dietary and other purity regulations were practised by the Pharisees and the Essenes, and were not enjoined on the whole people; they were originally intended only for the priests who served in the temple. In time synagogues emerged, in the Diaspora at first, it would seem, but also throughout the land, where prayer and Torah-study was conducted on the Sabbath, even though this was not stipulated in the Torah. However, it was only after the destruction of the temple in 70 CE that these places took on a sacral character, previously functioning as a general meeting place for local communities.

Regional variations operated among those who could be classed as belonging to the category of this common Judaism. Thus, for example, seasonal considerations in the different sub-regions determined the precise times for fulfilling various agricultural obligations. Likewise, the journey from upper Galilee to Jerusalem, which would take an average of eight days, would have made it impossible for all Jews to make the pilgrimage on three occasions during the year. But they were not thereby seen to be less Jewish because of that. Instead of the caricature of the Pharisees that one encounters frequently, their movement developed in order to make it possible for pious Jews to replicate in the home and the village the rituals associated with the temple in Jerusalem.

Insofar as we are aware, Jesus did not belong to any of the philosophies, though his early association with the Baptist may have meant that they both had been close to the Essene movement, and that he may have inherited their deep appreciation of the prophet Isaiah. The first three evangelists affirm that it was only after John's arrest that Jesus came into Galilee, thereby signalling a very different understanding of the imminent arrival of God's *basileia* or kingly rule from that which he had shared with John when they both were engaged in a ministry of repentance through baptism in preparation for the coming judgment of God.

The recognition in recent scholarship that Jesus was a Galilean has given rise to a lively debate as to how this regional perspective might have impacted on his Jewish identity and practice. For instance, in order to highlight his openness to non-Jews as well as Jews, the claim has been made that Galilee was very different to Judea with regard to practice, thus explaining his alleged 'liberal' attitudes. In its most extreme form this portrayal of Galilee as pagan territory has lead to the suggestion that Jesus himself was pagan not Jewish. The modern proposal that he was a Cynic teacher is not far removed from this egregious mis-construal of the Galilean Jesus. For at least a century before Jesus' birth, Galilee had been populated by Judeans who had moved northward after the Maccabeans had reclaimed what they perceived as the ancestral land. Indeed the names of Jesus' parents and siblings would suggest that they may well have belonged to such a lineage. Luke's story of Mary and Joseph going to Bethlehem for the Roman census (Luke 2.1) may thus be a faint echo of such a memory.

The Galilean background to Jesus' ministry is sometimes construed in such a way as to make him opposed to Jerusalem, once again putting him outside the pale of even a minimalist common Judaism. So how can we describe the relationship without minimizing Jesus' critique of the temple, so dramatically encapsulated in the temple episode (Mark 11.15–19)? There was plenty of precedent for the country prophet to challenge the centre, thereby putting his life in danger – from the prophet Jeremiah to a namesake of Jesus, Jesus son of Hananiah, who in 66 CE uttered woes on Jerusalem, the people and the temple, just prior to the outbreak of hostilities with Rome. Such manifestations of outrage at the luxurious lifestyle and values were directed in particular at the exploitative practices of the ruling elites. Amos, Isaiah, Ezechiel, and Jeremiah all railed against this ethos, without in any way being seen to be un-Israelite or anti-Jerusalem.

Within such a framework Jesus' well-known lament for Jerusalem is perfectly understandable: 'Jerusalem, Jerusalem, you who kill the prophets and stone those who are sent to you, how often have I desired to gather your children as a hen gathers her brood under her wings. See your house is left to you desolate' (Luke 13.34; Matt. 23.37). This is not the attitude of someone who is disinterested or hostile to the holy city. Rather it is the expression of a deeply frustrated, but also deeply caring prophet who has repeatedly sought to win Jerusalem over to his understanding of the demands of an inclusive justice and right living that God's kingly rule is now making on all Israel.

To construe this strained relationship with Jerusalem as though Jesus is reacting to the whole Jewish symbolic system associated with the temple, replacing it with some form of 'pure worship', is to ignore his Jubilee message of justice and care for all that was the foundation stone of his teaching. Furthermore, the social and political changes that had occurred in the Jerusalem priestly establishment during the Herodian period had led to feelings of alienation for many ordinary Jews, as several instances of protest during the first century CE demonstrate. Jesus' ministry, which offered God's blessings now for the poor and the marginalized, was a real catalyst for change in this regard. This dissatisfaction expressed itself differently in different circles. The Essenes for example saw themselves as a temple-community in the desert, while they awaited the day when God would build his own temple. As mentioned already, the Pharisees sought to extend the temple's symbolism to the home and village. Jesus preached that the active presence of God's kingdom was now occurring through his healings and teaching away from and independently of the temple. All this discontent was to erupt some thirty years later with the 'invasion' of the temple by country zealots, leading to the murder of the reigning high-priest and his replacement by a country peasant chosen by lot.

Once proper and full attention is given to the politico-religious context of Jesus' ministry both in Galilee and Jerusalem, it becomes abundantly clear that it was thoroughly Jewish, in the sense that it expressed the deepest yearnings of Jewish restoration and messianic hopes. This in no way diminished the special role that Israel was expected to play within the human family that had received the promise of Yahweh's blessing as the children of Abraham. Jesus reminded the Syro-Phoenician woman of this special place of Israel, while yielding to her pleas to heal her daughter (Mark 7.24–30). In this respect he conducted himself according to the best standards of his own tradition in treating the woman as a *ger*, that is, 'the foreigner in your midst', who was to be treated as an Israelite according to Pentateuchal law. Sabbath, food, and purity regulations were not dismissed in a cavalier manner by a Jesus who ignores his own tradition. 'These [i.e. "the weightier things of the law, mercy, justice and sacrifice"] you should have done, and not left the others [tithing, etc.] undone.' (Matt. 23.23; Luke 11.42). This aligns Jesus with other teachers who sought to encapsulate the various demands of the Torah in ways that were more readily accessible to ordinary people, outside the various scholastic groups that had emerged in the later second temple period.

II. Theological Reflections

Getting the contextual history correct is only one aspect of the quest for the Jewish Jesus, but it is indispensable if basic misunderstanding of what is meant by 'Jewish' as applied to Jesus is not to occur. In a highly influential 1954 essay the German theologian Ernst Käsemann formulated a criterion of dissimilarity, which sought to establish the uniqueness of Jesus by identifying what separated him both from his Jewish context and his Christian reception. As a historical principle this criterion had disastrous consequences for the Jewish Jesus. The image that application of this criterion was likely to give rise to would inevitably make him an un-Jewish figure, or at best only minimally Jewish. According to Käsemann and others who followed his lead, only those items of the tradition should be attributed to him that could be shown not to have been derived from either the Jewish context or the early Christian post-Easter development. Logically, this meant that Jesus would be seen as a stand-alone figure, who was neither Jewish nor Christian.

Theologically, Käsemann had hoped to show that by applying this principle to the Jesus tradition, he could establish continuity and identity between the proclamation *of* the historical Jesus and the proclamation *about* him, in a way that had been undermined by his teacher, Rudolph Bultmann.

But well intentioned though the move may have been, it seemed to ignore the importance of the resurrection experience of the earliest Jesus followers in terms of their coming to understand the real significance of Jesus. Had Käsemann not focused on Paul's preaching only, but considered instead the different portraits of Jesus that the Gospel writers felt free to develop in the post-resurrection period, he would have realized that it is not possible to reduce the Christ of faith to a single picture, and that this freedom of expression in early Christianity was an enrichment not a threat to Christian belief and practice.

Examination of these different portraits of Jesus in the canonical Gospels presents us with quite different aspects of Jesus' Jewishness. Yet each can be related to a particular context within the fraught situation of various groups of Jesus followers in their relationship with other branches of Judaism, all of which were also experiencing traumatic changes in both the pre- and post-revolt conditions of the late first century CE.

Thus, Mark's Jesus seeks to reassure followers of Jesus both from a Jewish and non-Jewish background (cf. 3.7–8) that the destruction of the temple by the Romans does not mean that God has once more abandoned Israel, as had happened at the time of the Babylonian captivity. They are not to follow false messianic hopes but await the return soon of the triumphant Son of Man, who will gather his elect.

Matthew's portrait is more polemical, especially against the scribes and Pharisees, who are said to teach but not to observe their own teaching. Yet the Jesus he presents is thoroughly Jewish in colouring. He is deemed to have been the Davidic Messiah from his birth, authenticated by various appeals to scriptural proof. Five collections of his teaching punctuate the narrative, reminiscent of Moses' five books of the Pentateuch. This teaching is at once thoroughly Jewish in that it is based on the law and the prophets, and yet at the end of the Gospel the disciples are directed to make disciples of all the nations. The destruction of Jerusalem seems to have receded somewhat in its immediacy by comparison with Mark. Instead the author has the confidence to claim that the destruction of the city was God's punishment for a recalcitrant people and that a new people, made up of Jews and gentiles, has replaced them as the true Israel. It is generally recognized that the sharpness of this polemic, though transposed back on to the life of the historical Jesus, in fact reflects the situation of the Matthean church, which sees itself in competition with emerging rabbinic Judaism in the late first century, possibly in Antioch.

Luke, also, is far removed from the destruction of the temple, which he treats not as an apocalyptic catastrophe, but as an historical event in the past (21. 20–4). His focus is on writing an apologetic account of the ministry of Jesus, whom he describes as a prophet of social justice, who was tried by the Romans on the charge of stirring up the people to insurrection, but was found innocent both by Pilate and by Herod Antipas. It was the Jewish leaders who insisted on his condemnation, even though the people had hoped that he was the one who would 'redeem Israel' (24.21). Behind this picture one suspects a desire to absolve Christian followers of Jesus in the cities of the Mediterranean world from any allegations of being subversive, and at the same time to provide them with ways of answering counter-charges emanating from the various synagogue communities in those cities, as Luke presents the situation in his second volume, Acts of the Apostles.

John's Gospel also builds on the picture of a Jewish Jesus, who as the *Logos* Incarnate has come to his own, but has been rejected by them. Jesus is the hidden presence of God, which traditionally was associated with the temple, That explains why the Johannine narrative is built around Jesus' presence in the Jerusalem temple at all the major feasts, declaring that he is the fulfilment of the symbolic rituals of the different festivals. The Jews are portrayed as the implacable opponents of Jesus throughout the work, and this opposition seems to be focused on whether or not his followers will be put out of the synagogue. It is generally accepted that these hostile exchanges between the Johannine Jesus and the Jews reflect the tensions that the community standing behind this corpus of writings, often described as the Johannine School, were experiencing with fellow non-messianic Jews. The very sharpness of the exchanges indicates just how close the two groups in fact were.

This brief overview of the different portraits of Jesus in the four Gospels indicates at once how dependent all the accounts are on the Jewish world of Jesus, and yet how vigorously each makes claims about him, giving rise to strident disputes with other Jewish groups. The opponents can be the scribes from Jerusalem (Mark), the scribes and Pharisees (Matthew), the chief priests and leaders (Luke), or simply the Jews (John). On the other hand, Jesus is the secret messiah who will return soon as Son of Man (Mark), the messianic teacher who fulfils the law and the prophets (Matthew), the prophet of social justice (Luke), and the incarnate *Logos*, the manifestation of the divine presence (John). Clearly, all these portraits cannot be collapsed into one picture and labelled 'the Jewish Jesus', especially when they are compared with the figure that was sketched out in the earlier section of this paper.

How can this polemical and pluralist picture best be appropriated today in ways that are not offensive to Jews who are sincerely interested in dialogue but who find the Christian portrayal of the Jewish Jesus to be both troubling and offensive? Are we faced with the dilemma as formulated by Rosemary Reuther, namely, that all christological claims are inherently anti-Jewish? Perhaps this is one instance where the figure of the historical Jesus can act as a safeguard against triumphant Christianity continuing to express its claims that are a-historical and therefore distorted. The search for the Jewish Jesus, once it is conducted within the parameters of contextual plausibility rather than those that emphasize uniqueness and difference, can be a good starting point for dialogue. After all, nowhere in the gospel tradition does Jesus claim to be the messiah, even when others proclaim him as such. 'You say that I am' was his reply to Pilate when the question was posed to him at the trial. The implications of that reply are that living the messianic life was for him more important than titles or claims. God will decide the future. Jewish and Christian explorers seeking the shared truth that they believe their different traditions have in common, despite all the distortions of the centuries, will do well to take this stance of the Jewish Jesus' as their starting point.

For further reading

Pope Benedict XVI (Joseph Ratzinger), _Jesus of Nazareth_, Eng. trans., New York and London: Doubleday, 2007.

Daniel Boyarin, _Border Lines, The Partition of Judaeo-Christianity_, Philadelphia: University of Pennsylvania Press, 2004.

David Flusser (with R. Steven Notley), _The Sage from Galilee. Rediscovering Jesus' Genius_, Grand Rapids, Michigan: Eerdmans, ⁴2007.

Sean Freyne, _Jesus a Jewish Galilean. A New Reading of the Jesus Story_, London and New York: T. and T. Clark International, 2004.

Susannah Heschel, _Abraham Geiger and the Historical Jesus_, Chicago: Chicago University Press, 1998.

Amy Jill Levine, _The Misunderstood Jew, The Church and the Scandal of the Jewish Jesus_, New York: HarperCollins, 2006.

E. P. Sanders, _Judaism: Practice and Belief, 63 B.C. – 66 A.D._, London: SCM Press, 1992.

Geza Vermes, _Jesus the Jew_, London: SCM Press, 1983.

Jesus: Genuinely Human

ANDRÉS TORRES QUEIRUGA

The christological mystery interweaves the basic strands of Christian theology. Understanding of the humanity–divinity relationship marks the way we grasp and experience our faith to a very profound extent. Simplifying to extremes, it appears as a double movement. First, the fact and manner of Christ's humanity form the basis of an *inductive ascent* toward confession of faith. Then, his divinity takes pride of place, becoming the basis of a *deductive descent* through which to interpret the humanity, tending to obscure it or even annul it. Understanding the reasons for this movement and showing the need to re-balance it, affirming his divinity *in and from* his humanity, are the prime concerns of this article.

I. From real humanity to deduced humanity

This process of inversion was undoubtedly inevitable, but its consequences were transcendental. From preacher, Jesus was turned into what is preached. The religious-cultural environment and apologetic requirements concentrated attention on the metaphysical study of his divinity, and, increasingly, this determined the understanding of his humanity: not *how* Jesus really *was*, but *how he must be* as the manifestation of divinity. The initial process was the move from a discovery (*that* Jesus exists) to a surprise (*how* he exists), ending with a revelation of his divinity (*who* he is in order to exist in this way). It was then turned upside-down, moving from the *who* to the *how* and at its most extreme (Docetism) even coming to question the *that*. This met with resistance, particularly within the Judeo-Christian environment, and the Gospels were surely produced to restore the balance – which is then upset in John.[1] The true humanity receded into the shadows: the intricate theological controversies show that at one extreme 'the "normal life" of the earthly Jesus had to appear as intrinsically miraculous'.[2] In fact, alluding to the two great champions of his divinity, it can be said that for

Athanasius the incarnate Word 'is not a human being'[3] and that Hilary is 'subtly Docetist'.[4] Chalcedon then needed to restore the balance after Ephesus: *'verus Deus'* but also *'verus homo'*.[5] An unstable balance. Neo-Chalcedonism showed that religious culture continued to stress the divinity at the expense of the humanity. Many people, in fact (and still today), developed an imagery that Karl Rahner characterized as crypto-Monophysitism.

Fortunately, this was not the whole story. Devotion never lost the sense of Jesus' humanity. The Gospels continued to be read, with their actions, their affections, their compassion and passion. Spirituality went on being nourished by these: it was not by chance that Thomas à Kempis protested against the 'types and species' of the scholastics and proclaimed the 'imitation of Christ'. Biblical criticism, breaking with literalism, and historical criticism, uncovering the cultural conditioning of dogma, combined with a culture that upheld the autonomy of the secular sphere and the integrity of humanity, brought a sense of urgency to recuperating Jesus' humanity, and provided new tools with which to do so.

Modern christology might be interpreted as an attempt to reverse the reversal, turning back to the beginning: re-treading 'the path of the apostles' (Schillebeeckx). We have to do christology 'from below', in a radical sense: redeeming the humanity and thereby reaching the meaning of the divinity. A difficult undertaking, as Albert Schweitzer showed – and a risky one, as the numerous errors and condemnations still occurring demonstrate. But it is a necessary, possible, and fruitful task, as the magnificent christologies of our times prove: they may be open-ended and incomplete, but they are certainly the best in Christian history.

Theoretical difficulty and 'epochal necessity' define the current profile of the problem of christology: rethinking what has been achieved in tradition and translating it into a new cultural paradigm.

II. Jesus, really and qualitatively human

The humanity of Jesus forms an essential point of departure: not just 'that' he is truly human, with no crypto-Monophysitisms, but 'how' he is human, so that we can read the revelation of his mystery and ours in that.

(a) Recovering the 'what': Jesus' humanity as grammar of his revelation

Since Chalcedon, express denial of Jesus' humanity has been ruled out. But it can still be said that, with so many mythic and falsely divinizing theories in existence, he is actually 'inhuman', alien to our history, which seeks and hopes, suffers and trusts, faces up to temptations and doubt, grows and matures over time. We all recall a Jesus with infused knowledge and wisdom, who knew everything (even while still in the womb), who did not suffer 'in the depths of his soul'; one who doubted, prayed, or questioned only to set an example, since he had no need to; who never made a mistake and who performed spectacular miracles, who expressly claimed to be the Messiah, the Son of God, God. . . . As a result, people competed to stress everything that made him different from us, from his miraculous birth to a sinlessness that allowed no limitations or defects of any kind.

This was a well-intentioned way of confessing his divinity. But it did so *not by studying it and learning it* in his real humanity but *by deducing it and imposing it* from what – by our standards – Jesus *must have been* in order to be able to be divine. This deduced humanity appeared to be fused with confession of faith: questioning it meant questioning the faith, leading to instinctive rejection and condemnation by the authorities. This was a profound reversal: a too-human interpretation was imposed in the name of faith, obscuring the true humanity of the Lord. This has been a permanent temptation: even in the Gospels Jesus 'rebuked' the apostles (Luke 9.55) and called Peter 'Satan' (Matt. 16.23).

The fears and opposition can be explained by the fact that what was at stake was sacred, and so it was not easy to make a change. But this is why a change 'must be' (*dei*) brought about *in the name of faith* and in openness to conversion. There is no avoiding the passage of time and a laborious apprenticeship. Rahner caused a scandal when he spoke of Jesus' a-thematic and progressive consciousness: cultural maturation has shown him to be 'clearly coherent' with the gospel accounts. Today the scandal is that anyone should be scandalized by this evidence. To persist in what we have learned, taking no account of advances in research, inevitably leads to viewing any renewed vision as heretical: whether in regard to the infancy narratives or christological titles, the raising of Lazarus and apparitions and the empty tomb. This disguises the fact that the real scandal, in a 'critical age' (Kant), is to make the faith incredible in the face of mounting historical evidence. This evidence, accumulating unstoppably, is uncovering the very specific humanity of a

Galilean Jesus, taking part in the social and religious movements of his people and his period – a 'Mediterranean peasant', a 'marginal Jew'.

Such facts are not a mere historical curiosity, since they make up the precise scenario *in which* the real Jesus is revealed: not through a theoretical gnosis but through 'everything to do with his presence and his manifestation of himself' (DV 4). There is nothing more anti-Christian than instinctive fear of new discoveries; rather, trusting in 'the self-evidence of the figure' (von Balthasar), our correct approach should be one of thankful openness, as each new feature enriches the *grammar* of our reading of his revelation. His contemporaries had direct experience of Jesus; he comes to us through interpreters. The deep meaning of inquiry into the 'historical Jesus' consists precisely in moving beyond this interpretation in order to attain, through it, the *same experience* and to interpret it in *our* culture. The experience generated the text; the text allows access to the experience. A critical approach to the text may look like pride; in reality it is the humblest of tasks. It may appear threatening, but the more it uncovers, the richer and truer will be the grammar in which we read the christological mystery.

(b) Learning the 'how': the mystery of Jesus reveals our mystery.

Speculation 'from above' took little account of Jesus' humanity. History is turning back to it, affirming its reality and emphasizing the importance of its manner. Made from the same clay as us, 'born of woman' (Gal. 4.4), Jesus reveals the ultimate meaning of our lives as rooted in the mystery of God. This is stated in one of the most luminous texts of the council: 'In reality it is only in the mystery of the Word made flesh that the mystery of humanity truly becomes clear' (GS 22). Discussions about 'natures' and 'hypostases' had their historical justification, but they parcelled out theological reflection, preventing it from focusing on the decisive element: how Jesus was and lived, so that we can decipher how we are and should live ourselves *in* his words, actions, and attitudes. Not even *kenotic* theologies, which may represent an advance in respect of the 'what', have always escaped the danger of speculations that obscured the 'how'.

Spirituality, I repeat, understood this better, and every life-giving movement in the Churches has drawn its nourishment from imitating and following the way Jesus was and lived. Their various accents were drawn from discoveries of new dimensions: *devotion moderna*, Ignatian exercises, revision of life, liberating following. In Jesus we learn that our existence is shielded by and enveloped in the infinite love and unconditional forgiveness of the *Abba* God; that trust in this God provides us with 'the courage to exist' (Tillich); that true humanity lies not in riches or power but in love, forgiveness, and service; that living and promoting community among our fellow human beings is the only legitimate way of believing in God.

Jesus' Beatitudes provide the inspiration, strength of conviction, and motivational force of the theologies of hope and of liberation. From them stem the option for the poor, the centrality of victims, the struggle against evil, and the promise of resurrection as definitive criteria for giving meaning to our being human in history. Jesus' actions and sayings call us to be a participatory Church, servant and committed to tolerance, freedom, and justice. The new quests for the historical Jesus, even if they do not always expressly recognize this, have their underlying justification here and are obeying a sure instinct of faith. (And I dare to think that even the unworthy deformations of some current writings demonstrate a hidden quest for a truly human Jesus.)

(c) God became man . . .

Accents are changing in relation to the mystery of God as well. Jesus is theocentric: his whole humanity, being revelation, becomes a 'parable' of God, steering our gaze not in the direction of metaphysical speculations but toward the 'different God' that his way of life makes clear. Sublime and transcendent, the object of deep adoration, this God is experienced as *Abba*. Reliance on his unrestrained love, which numbers every hair and does not exclude even wrongdoers (Matt. 5.43–8; Luke 6.35–6), trust in God's unconditional forgiveness, and, above all – as a strict result – his placing himself on the side of the poor, the persecuted, the excluded, move to centre stage. Taking the preaching of the prophets to the extreme, Jesus reveals that God's most urgent concern is not his 'glory' or 'being served' but the suffering of his sons and daughters. This is why God stands at their side and why, against all human violence and standards, they are 'blessed'. Believing in this God is not a matter of doctrinal pronouncement (Matt. 7.1), nor of wisdom and intelligence (cf. Matt. 11.25), nor of domination, exploitation, and tyranny (Mark 10.42–5; Matt. 20.25–8; Luke 22.25–7), but of compassion, help, and service: 'Come, you that are blessed by my Father . . . for I was hungry and you gave me food' (Matt 25.34–5). We need to open ourselves from here to the divine mystery, stating, in the genuine tradition, that

God is love and consists in 'the love that God has for us' (1 John 4.8, 16), and daring to draw the consequence that 'God's *only* concern in history is human beings', since God 'neither knows how nor wishes nor is able to do anything other than love'.[6]

Prior to any metaphysical-christological speculation, this is the primary and basic meaning of the 'incarnation': that God, after a lengthy work of preparation, in the Old Testament and in world religions, was able, thanks to the *humanity* of Jesus, totally open to God's love and call, finally to show us his truest and most defining face. Examining this humanity, accepting it with humility, allowing ourselves to be taught by it without imposing our criteria on it, is the basic task of christology. Only later and based on this can it legitimately move on to other things.

III. Toward the mystery of divine sonship: divinity 'in' humanity

The 'what' and the 'how' imposed the question of 'who'. The disciples asked it, and we need to ask it too: who is/was this man who 'speaks with authority', 'went about doing good', and 'loved to the end'? Our situation now is dialectical: it seeks an answer that, from historical realism, affirms Jesus' humanity without reservations, one that, with tradition, however, preserves the mystery of his divinity. This is an immense and open-ended task. Here only cruelly summary indications are possible.

(a) . . . that we might become God

The change of viewpoint proves decisive: it is not in the extra- or super-human that the mystery should be sought, but *in the human*. Pannenberg stated forcefully: 'If assertions about Jesus being God were to suppose a contradiction with Jesus' true humanity, then we should have to set confession of his divinity aside rather than doubt that Jesus was truly a man.'[7] And Leonardo Boff, stating that 'only God himself can be as human as Jesus was',[8] provides a good interpretation of the basic principle of Rahner's christology, that his human autonomy is in not inverse but direct proportion to the divine presence in him: 'Christ is human in the most radical manner, and his humanity is the most gifted with autonomy, the most free, not in spite of being assumed, but because it is assumed.'[9]

This represents a genuine change of paradigm. Spinoza warned against an incarnation conceived as 'transformation' (God would disappear and a man would appear): 'When some Churches add that God took a human form, I have expressly stated that I do not know what they mean; and even, truth to tell, that such a statement seems to me no less absurd than saying that a circle became a square.'[10] Elementary, but taking it strictly into account would require drastic revision of many treatises and put paid to a lot of theological rhetoric. Bultmann forcefully proclaimed the need for 'de-mythologization'; we should perhaps sometimes think this 'better than him' or even 'against him' (Ricoeur), but never moving back beyond his insight. Rahner fore-warned against applying a univocal 'is' to Jesus in his relationship to God, as if the two were parallel realities.

In effect, re-thinking the God-creation relationship as sameness-in-difference represents perhaps the *most crucial aspect* of a basic re-imaging of the christological mystery, already foreshadowed in the Lessing–Jacobi debate on Spinoza's *hen kai pan* and above all in the idealist quest. Christology has its place between the God separated from the 'dis-graced consciousness' and the Absolute that dialectically nullifies creatures. Von Balthasar himself stated: 'Maximus [the Confessor], with his christological philosophy of divinity-humanity, is Hegel's truth.'[11]

The change of paradigm can and must be undertaken. The danger stems not from affirming Jesus' humanity but from confining it positivistically, seeing no more than the 'carpenter's son' (Matt. 13.55; Luke 4.22) behind the historical data. Jesus' humanity is an icon, not an idol; a real symbol, not an empty sign. Indispensable as grammar (without literal meaning, symbolic meaning cannot exist), it opens up a unique and definitive mystery: *ep'eschatou*. Here reflection certainly requires us to slow down, to allow ourselves to be 'tutored' by tradition – not to take dictation from it but, as in certain university essays, in order to avoid already explored digressions and to concentrate on essentials. So a tutelage taken on critically, learning from that *experience* which, in 'less than two decades' – as Martin Hengel has stated[12] and Luis Hurtado, among others, has corroborated[13] – brought the first community to confess the christological mystery, manifested in a 'devo-tion' that, without denying Old Testament monotheism, expressed itself in symbols that introduced Christ into the inner being of the very Godhead and were later translated into conciliar dogmas.

The cultural shift rendered this double translation obscure. Paradoxic-ally, the first, that of the New Testament, often turns out to be clearer, owing to the spontaneity of its language. Present-day christology reflects this, insisting on the *religious* meaning of dogma and on *soteriology* as providing a

meaningful setting for christology. It does not, obviously, seek to deny dogmatic *truth* or its cultural legitimacy, but it does deny its indissoluble union
with its philosophical–conceptual mediation. What was said at the time was
thinkable then, but 'it would be even more puerile than rash to keep on
saying it today'.[14] We need to uphold what is essential: what, finally, Nicaea
sought to affirm against Arius is that 'nothing less than God was and is present and active in Jesus'.[15] Paul, so close to the beginnings, repeatedly uses
words that express the innermost structure of this concept: 'The God and
Father of our Lord Jesus Christ' (Rom. 15.6; 2 Cor. 1.3; 11.31; Col. 1.3; Eph.
1.3, 17), which J. D. G. Dunn explains as: 'Jesus is the *one* Lord exactly as,
and exactly because, God is the *one* God.'[16]

The identity between Jesus and God has to be confessed; the difference
between them has to be maintained. This is a difficult balance, which Paul
achieved thanks above all to his unshakable monotheism, but which the later
conceptual nature of the dogma rendered problematic. It would be theological suicide and epistemological ingenuousness to deny the truth of *what*
the dogma means, since, as Hegel wrote of the Trinity: 'If there is a meaning
in this Trinity, then we need to understand it. It would be bad for there to be
no meaning in what for two millennia was the holiest representation made by
Christians.'[17] But this meaning has to be rescued from a reifying literalism.
Tradition itself balanced 'God became man' by completing it with 'so that
man might become God'. The symbolism affects both parts of the statement. 'Become God' *derives from* the mystery of Jesus, but from him it
applies to all human beings, breaking all literalism, shedding light on
humanity with Jesus, but also shedding light from humanity on the statements made about Jesus: divine *in* his humanity.

It is within this tension, which has to conjugate two very diverse cultural
outlooks, that we today have to reshape interpretation of Jesus' divinity. The
founding experience sheds light on the depth of Jesus' humanity, but the
realism of this now makes up the grammar that, using *current concepts*, draws
us toward the meaning of the divinity of Christ.

(b) A seminal christology

I recall the favourable impression Schillebeeckx made on me by recognizing
the problems he had left open and unfinished at the end of his *Jesus*. I learned
that this was the fate of an honestly current christology: 'Beyond a first and
superficial impression, one soon comes to see that much, perhaps the best, of

his contribution is conveyed to us precisely through these difficulties. Nothing other could be expected, if a true attempt to open new paths is being made.'[18]

The present difficulties, fortunately, also open up new possibilities. The principal one should perhaps be sought in the very heart of the tension, deepening it in the direction of its true meaning. In Jesus-the-Christ we learn that the essential definition of what is human is not opposed to its radical rootedness in God. The reifying view that interprets divine difference in parallel with creaturely difference, in such a way that the 'other' of God implies negation of the creature (Feuerbach), inducing an inevitable 'dis-graced' consciousness, cast a shadow over tradition but never totally dominated it. From Aquinas' 'reducing the perfection of the creature is equivalent to reducing the perfection of divine power' (3CG 69.15) to Nicholas of Cusa's *non-aliud*, Christian understanding – contrary to Heidegger's onto-theological accusation – has appreciated that our rootedness in the God who creates-through-love affirms to the extent that it lays the foundations; it does not suppress autonomy: it consists in affirming it.

The infinite depth of this rootedness in which everything has its origin allows us to intuit Jesus' difference without denying his continuity with us: *filii in Filio*. The difference does not distance him; on the contrary it brings him closer and further unites him to us: it is *difference in continuity*, difference by 'intensification'. And this cuts all mythological and interventionist imagination off at the roots: by reversing the direction, it allows us to see Christ not coming down from above, like an external irruption into the world, but arising – like us, but in his specific difference – from the same divine source (remember Eckhart's profound considerations: created in the same being engendered as Christ). This lies at the root of the deep evocation of Rahner's christology, 'christology as anthropology finally reaching itself': this does not and cannot say everything, but perhaps it opens the most realistic route to inexhaustible meaning. It proclaims an urgent task for present-day christology.[19]

The divine character of Jesus, far from being threatened, opens its infinite depths, since the *how* and the *who* Jesus is strikes root in God's eternal decision. It is God himself, in God's *eternal* being and freedom, that is manifest in Jesus, as much in the 'economic' sense of historical manifestation as in the 'immanent' sense of the very divine being: Jesus is like that because from eternity God loves and determines *himself* as Father-of-Jesus. Jesus' *unique* character thereby appears as identical to divine sonship.

At the same time, solidarity does not deny ontology but gives it life in soteriology: *pro nobis*. Precisely because the difficulty in understanding Christ's 'difference' springs from his deep 'identity' with us, it also points to the focus of the greatest meaningfulness. I suspect that perhaps this is the announcement of a basic criterion for future christology: *The statements made about Jesus Christ acquire effective significance insofar as, in some manner and to due degree, they can also be made about us.* Pascal said as much: 'It is one of the great principles of Christianity that all that happened to Jesus Christ should come about in the soul and body of every Christian.'[20] Rahner continually implied this, seeing the hypostatic union itself as 'an internal stage in the totality of the gracing of spiritual creatures as a whole'.[21] And, let us recall, Vatican II takes this for granted, stating that our mystery is clarified in that of Christ: in understanding him, we understand ourselves; in understanding ourselves, we understand him (see GS 22).

This heated space of continuity/difference is the setting in which the unending task of christology will always move. It needs to uphold both, in an unceasing dialectic: the one and the other, the one criticizing and fertilizing the other. Jesus, recognized as brother and confessed as the Christ, is both 'pioneer' (*archechós*) and 'first-begotten' (*protótokos*): equal, but distinct; distinct, but equal.

Translated by Paul Burns

Notes

1. Cf. G. Theissen, *Die Religion des ersten Christen*, Gütersloh: Vanderhoek & Ruprecht, 2000, pp. 81.
2. G. Essen, *Die Freiheit Jesu*, Regensburh: Pustet, 2001, p. 55.
3. R. P. C. Hanson, *The Search for the Christian Doctrine of God*, Grand Rapids: Eerdmans, ²2007, p. 451.
4. *Ibid.*, p.; 501.
5. J. Moingt, *L'homme qui venait de Dieu*, Paris: Cerf, 1993, pp. 201–9.
6. This is a *leit-motiv* of my *Recuperar la creación*, Santander: Sal Terrae, 1997 (Galician original, Vigo, 1996).
7. *Fundamentos de cristología*, Salamanca: Sígueme, 1974, p. 235.
8. *Jesus Cristo Libertador*, Petrópolis: Vozes, 1976, p. 193.
9. *Curso fundamental sobre la fe*, Barcelona: Herder, 1979, p. 268.
10. Letter 73, to H. Oldeburg, in *Oeuvres complètes*, Paris: La Pléiade, 1954, p. 1283.
11. *Herrlichkeit* II/2, p. 655.
12. *Der Sohn Gottes*, Tübingen: J. C. B. Mohr & Paul Siebeck, p. 11.
13. Principally, *Lord Jesus Christ*, Grand Rapids: Eerdmans, 2003.

14. Moingt, *op. cit.*, p. 627.
15. R. Haight, *Jesus, Symbol of God*, Maryknoll, NY: Orbis, 1999, p. 299; cf. 288–99 and *passim*; Theissen, *op. cit.*, pp. 370–1, which ties it to the *Grundaxiom* of monotheism.
16. *The Theology of Paul the Apostle*, Cambridge: CUP & Grand Rapids: Eerdmans, 1998, p. 248; cf. chs 10–11. This is not negated by the linguistic and hermeneutical concomitancies with emperor worship – the emperor as 'Kyrios', 'Saviour', and 'Son of God' – but clarifies the process in a 'continuity by contrast'. This is amply analyzed by J. D. Crossan and J. L. Read, *In Search of Paul*, New York, HarperCollins, 2004: the same words transmit opposite experiences.
17. *Vorflesungen über die Geschichte der Philosophie* vol. 18, Frankfurt: Suhrkamp, p. 253.
18. 'El proyecto cristológico de E. Schillebeeckx', in *Repensar la Cristología*, Estella: Verbo Divino, 1996, pp. 61–156, here 107–8.
19. I have tried to do this in my books on *revelation* and *resurrection*: renouncing 'empirical interventionisms' is not to deny their salvific *reality*; on the contrary, it recuperates it critically on a deeper and more vital level.
20. Letter to M. and Mme Périer, 17 Oct. 1651, in *Oeuvres complètes*, pp. 497–8.
21. *Curso fundamental sobre la fe, op. cit.*, p. 241.

The Coming Kingdom or God's Present Reign

JON SOBRINO

I. The importance of going back to the Kingdom of God

For centuries neither christology nor the councils took the Kingdom of God preached by Jesus into account. Since its rediscovery at the beginning of the last century many christologies, especially those of a conciliar nature, have developed it as a central theme. What is at stake in approaching it now is, ultimately, knowing, hoping for, and cooperating to put God's wish for his creation into practice. We need to examine it with 'our gaze fixed on Jesus of Nazareth' and bearing the real course of the history of our world in mind.

The return to the Kingdom of God in theology has produced major fruits: a more Jesus-like faith and spirituality; a Church more closely resembling Jesus; and, here and throughout the developing world, a pleiade of 'prophets of truth', unmaskers of idols, and 'martyrs for compassion and justice'.

Making it central of course has its dangers, as with all human undertakings. Concentrating on the *Kingdom*, while underestimating other aspects of Jesus, can even lead us to forget *God*, to a sort of 'Christian atheism', as some have claimed: reducing Christianity, manipulating it for political and social ends, as others claim.

What I want to stress above all, however, is that keeping the Kingdom of God alive is essential if we are to lead decent human lives. And doing so is not easy. We are always threatened by the temptation to reject it or dilute it – as happens with anything relating to Jesus of Nazareth. In regard to Jesus, we have to uphold *confession of the sarx*, against the temptation to *Docetism*; his live of *love*, mercy, service – his whole praxis, in effect – against the temptation to *Gnosticism*; the folly of the *suffering servant*, against the temptation to *power*, including its sacred form of mediating salvation. We have to uphold *grace*, against the temptation to *hybris*. In the same way, we have to uphold the centrality of the *Kingdom* against the temptation to *privatize and*

44

spiritualize faith; to forget and cover up – and above all to produce – poor and victims, products of the anti-kingdom.

This is the basic standpoint from which I want to analyze what, in my view, is at stake concerning the Kingdom of God. We also have to start from the cruel reality of this world. We live in a 'seriously sick' society (Ellacuría), in a world 'sick unto death . . . in which it is murder if a child dies of hunger' (J. Ziegler). What is at stake is a worthy and just life for the poor. And for believers, God's honour, as well as the decency of our lives and actions, is at stake: 'Do not be the cause of God's name being blasphemed among the nations' is the very serious warning given five times in the Bible. Meanwhile, we are faced with the task of making the Kingdom grow, so that, on seeing it, 'his name may be glorified'. This is not just one more task, and it should not leave us in peace.

II. The basic premise: God's creation and desire

The God of Christianity is a God who creates a reality distinct from himself and who desires the good of his creation. While maintaining his transcendence, God himself is involved in this design of goodness. If I may be allowed to speak boldly: 'As it goes with creation, so it goes with God'. Tradition expresses this beautifully: '*gloria Dei vivens homo*', Ireneaus said. And many centuries later Archbishop Romero gave this phrase a historical context: '*gloria Dei vivens pauper*' – words that are not just literary but theological, since they introduce the *overcoming of non-life* (which the poor and the victims are) into the glory of God. And they introduce *partiality*: God does not rejoice in everything to an equal degree. The Kingdom of God will not be an abstract, universal, and timeless *utopia*; it will be life for the poor.

This brings us to the basic mystery of God: a God who freely decides not simply to be God and who establishes a positive relationship, of love, with his creation. This is the mystery in the strong sense given it by Rahner, who added: 'the mystery remains mystery eternally'. The subject of 'Jesus and the Kingdom of God' has to be situated within this greater mystery.

Taking this mystery seriously also brings a methodological outcome: the path to follow to understanding it has to be *mystagogical*. Exegetical and theological analysis is not enough, nor are magisterial formulations, if their understanding is not somehow soaked in the *mystery of God and the mystery of the reality* in which we live, and in which *God* dwells.

III. The Kingdom of God in the tradition of Israel

Jesus did not start with a blank sheet; he inherited the faith of Israel, in which God's plan for his creation came – late – to be expressed as the *Kingdom of God*. Israel went through innumerable misfortunes but, through its faith in God, kept alive its hope in *God's passage through history*. Inspired by the language of surrounding peoples, it formulated this as the *kingship*, the *reign* of God. And it understood this in a precise manner: 'He will judge the world with righteousness, and the peoples with his truth' (Ps. 96.13; cf. Ps. 72). In thematic terms, the reign of God 'transforms an unjust historico-social situation into a different, just one, in which solidarity reigns and no one will be in need (cf. Deut. 15.4)'.[1] Here are its essential elements:

Primordial compassion. Liberation from slavery and death. The passage of a liberating God. God's creation has often been damaged in history. The life of some – the majority – has been threatened and destroyed by minorities – and still is being today. This is a direct assault on God's glory. The *reign* of God will therefore bring wellbeing, but of itself and essentially it will bring liber-ation: God passes through the world to free a people from oppression and death so that it may have life. This is a compassionate God who is not con-cerned with himself. This essential compassion is fundamental to liberation theology – as compassion is fundamental to the political theology of J. B. Metz.

J. L. Segundo, dealing with the spiritualization of the liberation narrated in Exodus,[2] which would make the basic purpose the foundation of the people of God and the establishment of the alliance on Mount Sinai, insisted that in the most ancient sources – Jahwist, Elohist, Deuteronomic – 'there is not a trace of this supposed purpose'.[3] The purpose is that an oppressed people should have life and live as a people, and the Kingdom of God should be understood from this starting point. It has a dimension of *economic* life too, in the sense that it makes the *oikos*, the central nucleus of living, possi-ble. And it will be the fruit of primordial compassion.

Partiality. A reign that favours the poor and victims. The partiality of God for the poor is implicit in what has been said. But we need to analyze what is meant by 'poor' at various moments in history (it is to the credit of Latin American bishops that they did this at Puebla in 1979, Santo Domingo in 1992, and Aparecida in 2007) and furthermore what is common to all of these: life is a heavy burden for the poor, and they cannot take it for granted. The poor, too, are also those who normally have all the powers stacked against them. Poor and oppressed are virtually interchangeable terms.

Faced with this situation, God – first and foremost – takes the side of the poor and victims. Puebla put it in succinct terms: 'made in the image and likeness of God to be God's children, this image is darkened and even tarnished. . . . [Whatever the moral or personal situation in which they find themselves] God takes on their defence and loves them' (n. 1142).

This partiality is shown in God's passage through Israel. In the prophets, God does not call the whole of Israel 'my' people but only those who are oppressed within Israel.[4] The *confessio Dei* is found in the exclamation, 'in you the orphan finds compassion'.[5] Psalm 82, which J. D. Crossan calls the basic text for the whole of Christian life,[6] shows God in the divine council, instructing the other gods to 'give justice to the weak and the orphan; maintain the right of the lowly and destitute' (v. 3).

This partiality can leave our reason uneasy, although it should not do so. Theology has defended the universal *saving* will of God as obvious; faced with evident disparities, however, Rahner insisted: *voluntate tamen inequali*. This brings us up against the mystery of God: the salvation of a St Teresa of Avila and also of apparently mindless cretins. It is certainly the case that, where the poor and victims are concerned, reason can find this partiality somewhat more reasonable. But in any case, *God is like this*. As J. Jeremias said, the essential feature of the Kingdom is 'the offer of salvation Jesus makes to the poor . . . The kingdom belongs *only* to the poor.'[7]

Kingdom of God and People of God. In Israel, the people of God are the Kingdom of God. There will be no people without Kingdom and no Kingdom without people. 'Kingdom (of God) and people (of God) refer immediately to the complete historicity of God's relationship to us and ours to God.'[8] This means that the Kingdom of God has an essentially *social* dimension. Over time, the *person* gradually acquired more importance, and God's course was seen also as moulding persons. With Jesus' coming this becomes clear: God's plan is for every human being to become sons and daughters in the Son.

Note that the Kingdom is corellative to people: the people should act like the God who has shown them compassion and set them free. They should be people who work justice, who liberate: there are to be no more needy among them; they are to share the fruits of the land with outsiders, orphans, and widows (see Deut. 15 and 26; Lev. 19). By acting in this way, Israel will give justice to the poor, and the Kingdom of God will reign in their midst.

Seen in this way, the choice of Israel does not confer a privilege over other nations. It is rather a serious responsibility, and it is important to see it as such, since the concept of being 'the chosen' always entails great dangers – for the Church too. The Old Testament has no problem in stating that God has also, gratuitously, liberated the Ethiopians, the Philistines from Caphtor, and the Arameans from Kir (Amos 9.7ff), and even the Egyptians.

Mediators of God's passage through history. The philosophical tradition speaks of secondary causes. Religious traditions speak of angels, intermediaries between God and human beings. Christianity confesses the mediator by definition, Jesus Christ, the only-begotten Son, sharing in the very reality of God. In Israel, mediators are such out of *affinity* with the reality of God, not out of duty, so to speak. The just and compassionate, those who liberate and speak truth on behalf of the oppressed and against the oppressor, mediate God. They do so not from any sort of worldly 'power', always prone to instruct and subject, but because they are empowered by the 'power' of the Spirit, enabling them to form others in freedom. Therefore, those who belong to the institutional establishment should, above all, replicate God's compassion and partiality: 'The king's justice . . . does not consist primordially in issuing impartial verdicts, but in the protection it affords to the vulnerable and the poor, to widows and orphans.'[9] The bearers of salvation are above all the poor, the simple, the insignificant – not the powerful. Of all the kings, only two, Hezekiah and Josiah, stood up well to the judgment of the prophets: 'He judged the cause of the poor and needy; then it was well' (Jer. 22.16). Finally, a scandalous mediator appears: God passes through history in the mysterious figure of the Servant. Innocent, he suffers insults and death. He thereby takes on himself the sins of the world and, mysteriously, brings salvation.

This last consideration is essential in speaking of the Kingdom of God. It strives to make itself present in the midst of the anti-kingdom, but this has deep roots, which cannot be eradicated by struggling with them from outside, as it were, but have to be tackled from within, taking evil – the sin of the world – on oneself until one is crushed by it. This is salvation as *redemption*, which presages Jesus of Nazareth. And it hints at the greater mystery: in his passage through history, God passes through the cross of Jesus – scandal and folly, but salvation.

The eu-topia of the shared table. Israel lived on the memory of liberation and on a promise for the future. It never lost hope, and it always felt itself to be turned toward utopia. 'Kingdom of God' is, as is well known, a late formulation of this utopia, which was understood in a progressively broader sense.

In his comprehensive vision of a new creation, Isaiah wrote: 'They shall build houses and inhabit them; they shall plant vineyards and eat their fruit. They shall not build and another inhabit; they shall not plant and another eat. . . . Before they call I shall answer. . . . The wolf and the lamb shall feed together. . . . They shall not hurt or destroy on all my holy mountain' (65.21–5). Putting this in more anthropological and personal terms, Ezekiel wrote: 'I will remove from your body the heart of stone and give you a heart of flesh' (36.26). And Jeremiah understood it as the absolute closeness of God: 'I will put my law within them, and I will write it on their hearts; and I will be their God, and they shall be my people' (31.33).

This fullness should not, however, lead to forgetting what came first: everything starts with God's compassion for some slaves. And thinking of slaves, we need to understand properly the sense in which we can call – or not call – the Kingdom *ou-topia*, meaning something so exalted that there is no place for it, in the sense of Plato's Republic or Thomas More's Utopia, or the earthly paradise, or the universal resurrection of the dead.

In the situation our world is in, it would be better understood as *eu-topia*, the 'least-greatest' that Romero discussed with Leonardo Boff at Puebla: 'We need to defend the least, which is God's greatest gift: life'. And the hope of the victims clings to that. This *eu-topia* comes into being sometimes in modest forms. The poor are experts in suffering, but they do not give in to sadness; they have a capacity for organizing themselves and producing signs of the Kingdom of God. They celebrate it in community and, like Jesus, around a table. The shared table is still the great sign.

IV. Jesus and the Kingdom of God

Turning now to Jesus and the Kingdom, let us start with Peter's words: 'he went about doing good and healing all who were oppressed by the devil, for God was with him' (Acts 10.38). Jesus prayed for the coming of the Kingdom, and the Kingdom gave the sense of God's Fatherhood, an absolutely central experience specific to him, without which he cannot be understood. And, effectively, he declared it to be the ultimate thing: human beings should seek first the Kingdom of God 'and his righteousness' (Matt.

6.33), which some take to mean mere inner rectitude and others takes as the Old Testament concept of justice. In brief: Jesus believed in a God who *reigns*, for the sake of the *poor*, and the *people* themselves should serve the same ends. This faith was his *hope* and his *utopia*, and this was what he worked for.

Jesus' being and actions in the service of the Kingdom of God. Jesus both proclaimed the Kingdom and brought it definitively into being. But two points need clarifying: (1) His actions, such as his miracles, are 'signs' of the Kingdom, or 'petitions', as González Faus calls them, but they are not the whole of the Kingdom. This does not diminish their importance, since they point to the direction the Kingdom will take (life, peace, freedom, dignity) and generate hope that the Kingdom is possible, since the anti-kingdom can be conquered. (2) Jesus appeared to be related essentially to the Kingdom, but this relationship is not complete identification. Asking for the Kingdom to come (Matt. 6.10) is not the same as asking for Jesus to come; casting out demons in God's name (Luke 11.20) is a sign that the Kingdom of God has come, not that Jesus has come.

This does not take away from Jesus' importance in establishing the fullness of the Kingdom, especially after his resurrection. When Paul defines the Kingdom as 'righteousness and peace and joy in the Holy Spirit' (Rom. 14.17), he is not referring to the person of Jesus Christ, but he can be taken to be referring to what happens when human beings live *in tô Khristô*. Equally, that 'God may be all in all' (1 Cor. 15.28) does not refer to the person of Jesus Christ, but the final plenitude will come about on the basis of Jesus' self-giving to the Father.

The reign of God and Jesus of Nazareth, each as an entity, are central to the New Testament, but they are not the same thing. 'Reign' denotes a *social collective*; Jesus of Nazareth is *a person.* But the two are essentially related. Perhaps the first Christians saw the coming of Jesus as bringing new possibilities for creation, that this was now shot through with a presence of God, which meant that everything tended toward compassion, conciliation, truth. How far history was to confirm this doxological conviction is another matter.

The foundational mercy of a non-egocentric, non-self-centred God. This is a central intuition that emerges from the Gospels, even if not in passages that deal with the Kingdom of God. Jesus tells us who this non-self-centred God, inclined toward human beings, is. His *foundational mercy* sometimes appears in Jesus' parables and actions; at other times he tells us, indirectly but effectively, what God wants from us.

Matthew 25 shows Jesus deciding everything on compassion for the *poor and the weak*. He twice quotes Hosea 6.6.: 'I desire steadfast love and not sacrifice' in defence of the weak – of publicans in Matthew 9.13 and of the hungry in 12.7. This is more important to God than legal purity or keeping the sabbath (and private property). And in Matthew 5.23 he turns to reconciliation with one's brother, more important than the offering on the altar. Mark 2.28 and parallels solemnly declare that 'the sabbath was made for humankind and not humankind for the sabbath'.

In the three Synoptics Jesus treats love of God and love of neighbour as equal, which is already scandalous enough, but more scandalous is the fact that in the original version of Mark, love of God was not mentioned. According to the reconstruction made by Boismard, the earliest text says only that the greatest commandment is 'you shall love your neighbour as yourself; there is no other greater commandment'.[10] And in fact the expression 'love God' appears only three times in accounts of the principal commandment (Mark 12.30; Mat. 22.37; Luke 10.27) – also in Luke 11.42 (parallel of Matt. 23.23, where 'love of God' is not mentioned). Jesus answers the rich young man (Mark 10.17–22 par.) by listing his obligations to his neighbour, not to God. Paul takes the same line: 'For the whole law is summed up in a single commandment, "You shall love your neighbour as yourself"' (Gal. 5.14); 'for the one who loves another has fulfilled the law' (Rom. 13.8).

The paucity of texts on 'love of God' is surprising, and John's theology explains it with total clarity. He proclaims what we might call the *founding surprise* of the Christian faith: 'God has loved us first' (1 John 4.10). The proof of this is that God sent his Son, and the reason for this is that 'God is love' (4.8). What is most surprising, however, is his conclusion: 'since God loved us so much, we also ought to love one another' (4.11). God, founding love, places himself on one side. God loved us and wants us to do likewise, by being lovers of our brothers and sisters, as he is. 'God created us creators', said Bergson. The Letter says the same in speaking of being *in* God and abiding *in* God (1 John 4.16).

It does not use the language of Kingdom of God, but it does present the deepest logic of God's plan: a kingdom for human beings. God is like this directly for the poor and victims. And this is what lies behind many of Jesus' parables and stories that start with, 'the kingdom of God is like . . .'.

Jesus went about doing God's work. 'God was with him', Peter says. Jesus is *the* mediator. He makes God present, being the only-begotten. In the terms used by tradition, this can be expressed in two basic ways: he is the one who *reveals God's truth* and the one who *does God's will.*

In the language of John's Prologue, he is *charis kai aletheia*. Both terms can be translated as 'grace and truth' (cf. 1.14; NRSV), but many have sought a translation that goes deeper into the reality of Jesus Christ: 'love and loyalty' (*Biblia Española*); 'love and faithfulness' (*Biblia Latino-americana*); 'compassion and goodness';[11] 'the Word full of merciful love and faithfulness';[12] 'faithful mercy, characteristic of the Divinity'.[13]

Priority is give here to *charis*, love, in carrying out the Father's work. And the same applies to the opposite: the devil is a 'murderer' and a 'liar' (John 8.44), and in that order. Jesus' course through the world consists in doing what the Father does (John 5.19). And what the Father does is cure a paralyzed man (John 5.2–18) and a blind man (John 9.1–40). In this sense, 'revealing God's truth' is 'doing God's work' – and certainly works of mercy. And so we end where we began: God is compassion for victims. Jesus proclaims and expresses God's truth in himself, obviously. But *first and foremost*, he makes God's love and compassion for the victims present. These are 'the signs of the Kingdom'.

Three final thoughts

1. The situation God's creation is in is catastrophic and cruel, and human beings should be ashamed of it. The scale of death in the Middle East and Africa is matched by 'collateral' deaths around the world, products of a commercial war in foodstuffs. The wealthy nations subsidize entire crops or meat production while the poor nations die of hunger. Fewer than ten transnational businesses control the seed markets of the entire world. This is the anti-kingdom. But, unobserved and with no interest from the powerful in making it known, there are many deeds of holiness, many shared tables, much of what the Father does, which is to cure the blind and the paralyzed. This is the Kingdom.

2. There are many christologies, and many of these are valuable. But there is a lack of radical appreciation of, and a failure to give due systematic centrality to, Jesus' *death on a cross*. The reason for this is that it is not situated historically in the socio-political conflicts of his time. Even Aparecida,

which was very positive in other ways, passed over 'why Jesus was killed'. Jesus is shown as supremely virtuous – with apologies for stating the obvious – but not as becoming directly involved in conflicts with those in power. This oversight is perhaps due to an unwillingness to face up today to the fact that the innumerable martyrs of the Third World were murdered at the hands of oppressors – and to face up to the latter. Looking the anti-kingdom in the face makes it easier to recapture the historical truth of the death of Jesus and of the martyrs.

3. Finally, let us go back to the beginning. The creator God, who rejoices in his creation, is, at the same time, himself joy for his creation, carrying it to its fullness, as the continuation of Ireneaus' phrase states: *'gloria autem hominis visio Dei'*. Archbishop Romero asserted the same: 'It is impossible to know oneself without knowing God. . . . Who could have told me, beloved brothers and sisters, that the fruit of my preaching today would be that each one of us went out to meet God and that we should live the joy of God's majesty and our littleness!'[14] 'To see God', 'to trust in God', 'to rest in God', as Augustine said, is one way of expressing the fullness of being human. The Kingdom can also show us something of what this God is: unconditional love, who does not terrify through his imposing majesty but produces joy through his loving closeness. 'Seeing him', 'letting oneself be welcomed by him', is a blessing for human beings. The language can only be tentative, and, please God, mystagogical. The Kingdom of God in no way distances us from the God of the Kingdom. It can make him closer and even more 'human'. This is what was made present by Jesus' course through this world.

Translated by Paul Burns

Notes

1. X. Alegre, 'El Reino de Dios y las parábolas de Marcos', *Revista Latino-americana de Teología* 67 (2006), 8.
2. See the 1984 Vatican Instruction on the theology of liberation, V, 3.
3. J. L. Segundo, *Teología de la liberación. Respuesta al cardenal Ratzinger*, Madrid, 1985, p. 63.
4. Cf. J. L. Sicre, *'Con los pobres de la tierra'. La justicia social en los profetas de Israel*, Madrid, 1984, p. 448.
5. H. Wolf, *Dodekapropheten* I, p. 304.
6. J. D. Crossan, *The Birth of Christianity*, New York, 1999, p. 575.

7. J. Jeremias, *Teología del Nuevo Testamento* I, Salamanca, 1974, pp. 133, 142, italics in the original.
8. I. Ellacuría, 'El pueblo de Dios', in *Conceptos fundamentales de Pastoral*, 1983, p. 843.
9. J. Jeremias, *op. cit.*, p. 122.
10. P. Benoît and M. Boismard, *Sinopsis de los cuatro evangelios* II, Bilbao, 1976, p. 329.
11. P. Miranda, *El ser y el Mesías*, Salamanca, 1973, p. 144.
12. M. E. Boismard, *Le prologue du saint-Jean*, Paris, 1953, pp. 80–95.
13. J. L. González Faus, *La humanidad nueva*, Santander, [6]1984, p. 330.
14. Homily, 10 Feb. 1980, in *ibid.* p. 370.

Salvation and the Cross

LISA SOWLE CAHILL

I. Traditional views of the cross and contemporary critiques

A widespread view of Christian salvation is that believers are saved through the sufferings of Christ, who endured death on a cross as a punishment for human sin. In this idea of salvation, whose origin is often attributed to the eleventh-century theologian Anselm of Canterbury, the cross of Christ is a substitute for the punishment humans deserve. By suffering in our stead, Christ satisfies the justice of God and reconciles God to us, so that we may enjoy eternal life instead of damnation. As will be explained below, this model of salvation was not really Anselm's. The model of 'penal substitution' appears as early as Origen, who saw Christ's death as a propitiatory sacrifice;[1] it is promoted and popularized by the Reformers, especially John Calvin;[2] yet it is not the tradition's exclusive or dominant model.

Nevertheless, the ideas that the dying Christ bears a punishment that God demands as a condition of atonement, and that the point of the incarnation is the cross, have a strong hold on Christian imagination and popular piety. In the words of one nineteenth-century Catholic author: 'Justice will wreak terrible revenge. Mankind will be given the part of least suffering; it is another – man in order to suffer, God in order to expiate sufficiently, man-God in order to mediate between God and man – who will bear all the weight of the divine vengeance . . . he is in the Garden of Olives, in torments under the weight of our sins and of his Father's justice.'[3]

For generations, Christians have worshipped the figure on the cross who so generously and innocently suffers death so that we might have life. By bringing to mind this function of Christ, the image of the cross evokes a strong identification with the depths of Christ's human suffering, and a profound gratitude to the Father for having given us the gift of his only Son.

In recent decades, this model of salvation through the cross has come under theological attack.[4] Edward Schillebeeckx protests, 'many existing theories of our redemption through Jesus Christ deprive Jesus, his message

55

and career of their subversive power, and even worse, sacralize violence to be a reality within God. First sin must be avenged and only then is reconciliation possible.'[5] Feminist and liberation theologians agree.[6] If violence is the means of redemption, then violence is God's will. God is an angry God, who demands that the innocent submit to unjust abuse and death. This is not a liberating image for women, or for any oppressed peoples. It is not a model of salvation that assures those who suffer that God is on their side.

Two alternative interpretations of the meaning of the cross do not see the cross *as such* as salvific. Both have gained substantial theological support. One interpretation is that the cross is not in itself the instrument of salvation, but the outcome of a life lived in union with God and in dedication to all whom society rejects. The cross is the price of truly embodying the gospel. Again Schillebeeckx: 'Jesus' death on the cross is the consequence of a life in radical service of justice and love, a consequence of his option for the poor and outcast, of a choice for his people suffering under exploitation and oppression. Within an evil world any commitment to justice and love is deadly dangerous.'[7]

A second alternative interpretation of the cross is that it represents not a punishment for sin but God's solidarity with those who suffer. And cross as solidarity must be linked with resurrection as vindication in order to bring redemption. In the view of Jon Sobrino, Christ on the cross identifies with the victims of history. Seen in the light of the resurrection, the cross represents the hope 'that justice be done to the victims of this world, as justice was done to the crucified Jesus' when he was raised from the dead.[8]

These critiques of traditional theologies of the atonement and the new perspectives they inspire lead us to an important question: How is it still possible, helpful, and valid for Christian theology today to see the cross as bringing salvation? What are the biblical and theological grounds of such a claim? What are its political implications? And what are its limits?

II. Criteria for Constructing Theologies of the Cross

This essay will propose that the cross is rightly seen as part of the salvific process, though not as its centerpiece. And soteriologies need not emphasize the cross. New Testament images and models of salvation are pluralistic; theologies of salvation should remain pluralistic, even if not all are equally authoritative. The letters of Paul contain a rich variety of metaphors for salvation in Christ, including atoning sacrifice (Rom 3.25, 5.8–9); ransoming from debt, captivity, or slavery (1 Cor. 6.14, 7.22); and recapitulation of human history through the entire life of Christ as the 'second Adam' (Rom 5.14–19; 1 Cor. 15.45–6). The Letter to the Hebrews draws on Jewish martyrological traditions, priestly sacrifice in the temple, and the liturgy of the Day of Atonement to portray the death of Christ as an 'expiation' for sin, in the sense of cleansing and purification of sinners (Heb 2.17, 9.22). As the biblical scholar James Dunn emphasizes, *'from the first the significance of Christ could only be apprehended by a diversity of formulations which though not always strictly compatible with each other were not regarded as rendering each other invalid.'*[9]

No one theological explanation will ever be adequate to what is ultimately a mystery, approached not only through theological analysis, but through narratives, liturgy, prayer, and other Christian practices. Therefore soteriologies that keep a central role for the cross are complemented by other models. Another approach is salvation as 'divinization' (*'theosis'*) through the incarnation. Eastern theology, pre-eminently the Cappadocian Fathers, emphasizes that the unity of divinity with humanity in the person of Christ enables human participation in the divine life.[10] Moreover, even within cross-centred soteriologies, there are numerous ways to theologize the cross. Variation expresses differences in experiences and needs of people in different cultures at different times; it is encouraged rather than excluded by the spare, paradoxical formulations of Nicaea and Chalcedon.

Despite differences in soteriologies and in theologies of the cross, it is possible to establish standards of adequate Christian speech about the cross and salvation. These are set by the nature of Christian experience and by criteria of theological adequacy following from it. What are the defining elements in Christian experience? First, in Jesus Christ, believers find a relationship to God, and reconciliation with God and others (atonement), both during Jesus' lifetime and after his resurrection. Theologies of the cross must represent this experience of healing and union authentically. Second, both the Gospels and historical research into first-century Christianity confirm the scandalous fact that Jesus died a cruel, unjust, and ignominious death, a death that was shocking and terrifying to his first followers. It was difficult to reconcile this death with faith in God, narrate it religiously, and explain it theologically. Struggling for answers, New Testament authors renegotiated familiar religious and cultural symbols, yielding a pluralism of responses still normative today.

Finally, the *content* of salvation is communicated by Jesus' own words and actions: his expressed relation to his Father in heaven (*'Abba'*), his ministry of the kingdom or reign of God, and his willingness to die for the gospel that he lived. What does the way of salvation (discipleship) look like concretely? The nature of the Christian life is known from Jesus' healing ministry, his table fellowship with sinners and outcasts, his parables of love, sacrifice, and service to those in need (Luke 10, Matt. 25), and his command in all four Gospels to demonstrate love of God by loving our neighbors as ourselves – and even loving our enemies (Matt. 5.38–48).

The experience of God and reconciliation, the scandal of the cross, and the gift of kingdom life define Christian identity and community. They must be formative in explaining Christ's death and its relation to our salvation. At least five criteria are implied by these foundational facts of Christian life. (1) Christ as saviour must be proclaimed as fully divine and fully human; (2) Christ's suffering must be explained without making God violent; (3) Christ must be portrayed as saving both the innocent and the guilty; (4) the efficacy of Christ's action *for us* must be explained; (5) salvation must be presented not only as spiritual but also as social and political.

(1) *Christ is fully divine and fully human.* Christians have always sought to comprehend the mystery of how someone who was clearly a human being, Jesus of Nazareth, can and does fully embody the reality of God. The limits of concepts and language make this a difficult task. Christological heresies result from refusal to live with the mystery, oversimplifying it so that it can be grasped by human understanding. One of the first great heretics, Arius, found it impossible to believe that Jesus is fully divine; in later times, people have found it hard to accept that Jesus is fully human, sharing human thoughts, emotions, physical experiences, and even limitations. The creeds do not *explain* the mystery of Christ's identity. They state simply that Jesus is no less than fully divine *and* fully human, however much that creates a conundrum for theological inquiry. According to the Council of Chalcedon (450), 'Our Lord Jesus Christ is one and the same Son, the same perfect in Godhead and the same perfect in manhood, truly God and truly man . . . like us in all things except sin.'[11]

Both the divinity and humanity of Christ are necessary to explain the cross theologically as effective for salvation. The most influential theology of the atonement, that of Anselm, attempts to account for both. Anselm proposed that Christ had to be fully human in order to make compensation for human sin; but Christ had to be fully divine as well, since no finite human being could rectify the injury done to God's honour by human disobedience.[12] The 'standard,' though inaccurate, reading of Anselm infers that he envisions God as implacable judge, demanding that an innocent man be punished to appease his anger.

This model of the atonement holds on to the humanity and divinity of Christ; it also explains the cross. But it fails to meet another criterion of an adequate soteriology:

(2) *Christ's suffering must be explained without making God violent.* Some recent interpretations of Anselm suggest that he did not in fact view the cross as substitutionary punishment.[13] Anselm does speak of God's 'honour' and of a 'debt' owed to God. However, Anselm, like the Bible, never says God needs to be reconciled to us; rather we need to be reconciled to God. The honour of God is not the personal status of an insulted potentate; it is God's creative, providential, ordering relation to creation. Someone 'dishonours God' when he or she disturbs 'the order and beauty of the universe.'[14] The debt owed is the restoration of harmony. This, not punishment, is why Christ must be both divine and human. Christ restores *human* obedience to God in the sense of complete and intimate unity with the divine love for creation. The cross is the price of Christ's unwavering determination to exist within this love and unity. Christ's suffering was 'inflicted upon him because he maintained his obedience,' and 'for no other reason than that he had maintained truth and righteousness unflinchingly in his way of life and in what he said.'[15] Simultaneously, in Christ, *God* enters the human situation, identifying completely with those who have disturbed it and consequently suffer. By uniting humanity with divinity, Christ heals and transforms human existence. The cross is the consequence of Christ's unity of natures within the sinful conditions of history.

(3) *Christ saves both the innocent and the guilty.* Contemporary theologies of liberation rightly portray the cross as God's saving and rectifying solidarity with sin's victims. This interpretation assures the oppressed and the powerless that God is on their side. Moreover, it turns the eyes of privileged Christians to the social effects of personal sin, to social structures perpetuating sin, and to the 'preferential option for the poor.' It is crucial to account theologically for the conversion and transformation of the oppressors.

The role of the cross as saving both innocent and guilty is captured brilliantly by Jürgen Moltmann, who recalls the pain and horror he felt as a young German prisoner of war. Drafted as a teenager, he did not realize Hitler's crimes against the Jews until pictures of the extermination camps were posted in the prison. He and others despaired, in shame and guilt.

Finally, reading a bible given to him by a chaplain, Moltmann realized that Christ died for him too. By his death, by his accompaniment of sinners all the way into utmost grief and abandonment, Christ transforms and 'divinizes' the most terrible corners of human existence. 'I summoned up the courage to live, at a point when one would perhaps willingly have put an end to it all. This early companionship with Jesus, the brother in suffering and the liberator from guilt, has never left me since. The Christ for me is the crucified Jesus.'[16] In this model, death is not as such the purpose of the incarnation, but death, a suffering death, follows from God's determination to be in complete solidarity with everything that is human 'except sin.' The presence of Christ with, to, and in sinners enables transformation and sanctification, guided by Christ's own ministry.

(4) *Christ's action is efficacious for us.* Christ lives and dies in complete solidarity with God and with human beings. His humanity is the vehicle of our incorporation into the divine life too. But the claim that 'in Christ' we receive 'grace,' uniting us with God, can sound like a theological abstraction. How exactly does the being of Christ become our being, the love of Christ become our own way of life? The answer to this question lies in the Church, as 'body of Christ' and the community where Christ's Spirit acts in life-changing power. The Church as body of Christ and community of the Spirit cannot be equated with any ecclesiastical form or liturgical ritual, though forms and rituals are necessary to mediate life in Christ's body as a historical reality across time. The Church is authentically Christian and effective when it moulds communities of believers that reflect, however imperfectly, the redeeming love of Christ in their mutual relations and their participation in 'the world' (1 Cor. 13).

Just as Jesus Christ and salvation are imaged in many ways in the New Testament, so is the Church. The nature of Paul's ministry compelled him to deal constantly with the nature and function of the Church, embodied in different communities to which he preached the gospel. Primary among Paul's metaphors for the Church is body of Christ (1 Cor. 12.12–24). 'But the church is not merely *like* a body. Rather, it has become one body in Christ because its members participate in the one Eucharistic body of Christ' (10.16–17). Paul presupposes that the local *ekklesia* participates in and belongs to the body of Christ because its members have been baptized into Christ's body (12.13) and share his eucharistic body (10.16).'[17]

What is the role of the cross as salvific in the Church? The prayers, liturgies, and moral practices of the Church form members in relation to God and fellow human beings. Church is the communal way of service, love, and joy, imbued by the theological virtues: *charity* as partaking in the divine nature, *faith* as trust in God and conviction of God's real presence, and *hope* as anticipation of new life already begun now. Joy, trust, and hope nourish the courage to confront and accept suffering when it is unavoidable in pursuing the kingdom and the gospel of good news to the poor. The cross does not give discipleship its primary contours, but it does inevitably characterize faithfulness in a broken and unjust world.

(5) *Salvation is not only spiritual, but also social and political.* In his recent book, *Jesus of Nazareth*, Joseph Ratzinger frames the gospel of Christ and the good news of the kingdom in a way intended to appeal to secular societies whose members have lost their sense of transcendence and their hope for a relationship to God. Ratzinger stresses the divine nature of Christ, and the possibility that through Christ human beings can come to know God in a personal way. Christ's sacrificial death, as the pre-existent Word of God, makes this possible. 'The incarnate Logos is the true "sheep-bearer" – the Shepherd who follows after us through the thorns and deserts of our life. Carried on his shoulders, we come home. He gave his life for us. He himself is life.'[18]

This treatment may meet a spiritual need of modern Western societies searching for a sense of the divine. However, it leaves out one key element in the meaning of the Kingdom of God as Christ portrayed and lived it: the preferential option for the poor. For Ratzinger, the Kingdom of God is present where Christ is present. What the Kingdom means is 'communion with Jesus' and with the will of the Father, and continuing life in Christ.[19] This depiction is true as far as it goes, but it is unfortunately devoid of any social content specifying what union with Christ means in relation to our neighbours and for our roles in society. Social action is indispensable to the Kingdom of God, as Jesus illustrated with the parable of the Good Samaritan. A travelling Samaritan helped an injured Jew, overcoming stereotypes and barriers prescribing enmity between them (Luke 10). This parable embodies the significance of the cross for the Christian life, representing one identifying with another's suffering, accepting the risk of compassionate action.

Conclusion

In the words of a Philippina feminist theologian, theories of Christ should never permit us to 'veer away from the ethics of accountability' to the concrete situations of human life. 'Christ-talk is Christology half done. It has to be practiced. Jesus has shown us how.' Christ is God-with-us who weeps with our pain, dances with us to celebrate our little triumphs over the many crosses in our lives, and leads us toward the fullness of life at the breast of the ultimate Mystery we call God.'[20] The cross is part of the way of salvation. Yet the cross does not or should not exalt suffering or image God as vengeful, angry, unmerciful, or unforgiving. The cross is redemptive because it is the transforming identification of God with all who are desperate, oppressed, or guilty, signalling the raising of all into divine love. The cross saves within a process of incarnation, resurrection, and the sending of Christ's Spirit.

Notes

1. Origen, *Homily on Leviticus*, I. 3, as cited in J. N. D. Kelly, *Early Christian Doctrines*, New York, Evanston, & London: Harper & Row, [2]1960), p. 186.
2. John Calvin, *Institutes of the Christian Religion*, Vol. 1, trans. Henry Beveridge, Grand Rapids, MI: Eerdmans, 1981, Book II. Chapter XVI. 2.
3. Abbé F. Maucourant, *La vie d'intimité avec le bon Sauveur*, Nevers, 1897, p. 23; as cited by Philippe de la Trinité, O.C.D., *What is Redemption?*, trans. Anthony Armstrong, O.S.B., New York: Hawthorn Books, 1961, p. 20.
4. For an overview, see Stephen Finlan, *Problems with Atonement: The Origins of, and Controversy about, the Atonement Doctrine*, Collegeville, MN: Liturgical Press, 2005; and Robert J. Daly, S.J., 'Images of God and the Imitation of God: Problems with Atonement,' *Theological Studies* 68 (2007), 36–51.
5. Edward Schillebeeckx, *Church: The Human Story of God*, trans. John Bowden, London: SCM Press, 1990, p. 125.
6. See, for example, Marit Trelstadt (ed.), *Cross-Examinations: Interrogating the Cross for Its Meaning Today*,Minneapolis: Fortress Press, 2006.
7. Schillebeeckx, *Church*, p. 125.
8. Jon Sobrino, *Christ the Liberator*, trans. Paul Burns, Maryknoll, NY: Orbis Books, 2001, p. 48. See also José María Vigil, organizer, *Getting the Poor down from the Cross: Christology of Liberation*, 2007, published online by the International Theological Commission of EATWOT (http://www.servicioskoinonia.org/LibrosDigitales/; accessed 6 March 2008).
9. James D. G. Dunn, *Christology in the Making: A New Testament Inquiry into the Origins of the Doctrine of the Incarnation*, London: SCM Press, 1989, p. 267.
10. See Anthony Meredith, *The Cappadocians*, Crestwood, NY: St. Vladimir's Seminary Press, 1995.
11. Kelly, *Early Christian Doctrines*, p. 339.
12. Anselm, 'Why God Became Man', in Brian Davies and G. R. Evans, *Anselm of*

Canterbury: The Major Works, Oxford and New York: Oxford University Press, 1998.

13. Richard W. Southern, *Saint Anselm: A Portrait in a Landscape*, New York: Cambridge University Press, 1990.
14. Anselm, 'Why God Became Man', Book I. 15.
15. *Ibid.*, Book I. 9
16. Jürgen Moltmann, *Jesus Christ for Today's World*, London: SCM Press, 1994, p. 3.
17. Frank Matera, 'Theologies of the Church in the New Testament', in Peter Phan (ed.), *The Gift of the Church; A Textbook on Ecclesiology*, Collegeville, MN: The Liturgical Press, 2000, p. 15.
18. Joseph Ratzinger, *Jesus of Nazareth: From the Baptism in the Jordan to the Transfiguration*, trans. Adrian J. Walker, New York and London: Doubleday, 2007, p. 286.
19. *Ibid.*, pp. 146–7.
20. Muriel Orevillo-Montenegro, *The Jesus of Asian Women*, Maryknoll, NY: Orbis, 2006, p. 200.

Opening up New History: *Jesus of Nazareth* as the Beginning of a New History

ERIK BORGMAN

There is clearly much to be learned from christology. But is there something new to be learned *in* christology? If one did not already, the reading of the first volume of Joseph Ratzinger's projected christology makes one wonder.[1] Much of what has been discovered and developed in theology in recent times is attacked because it differs from the traditional way of seeing and presenting the Christian tradition. This is all the more alarming because reading the first volume of *Jesus of Nazareth* is such a confusing experience.

I. Ambiguities in Ratzinger's book on Jesus

On the one hand one gets the impression that one is reading the personal meditations of an erudite theologian and rather traditional Roman Catholic *hierarch* – meditations to respect rather then to polemicize with, even if one does not agree with it, because they are so clearly personal in nature – but at the same time one seems to be reading the message hidden behind the recent measures and condemnations against theologians who have written on christology.[2]

The fact that the author of the book is identified in a double manner, as Joseph Ratzinger and Benedict XVI, adds to the confusion. The preface gives the impression that the double identification comes from the fact that parts of the book were written well before Ratzinger became pope. However, if the message is meant to be that 'this book is not at all a magisterial act, but the expression of my personal seeking of the "Lord's face" (Ps. 27.8)', as is also stated in the preface, and that therefore 'everyone has the liberty to contradict [it]', it would have been better had its author kept to the name Joseph Ratzinger only. As person and theologian he can claim the liberty to express his convictions and sensitivities, just like the rest of us – although, given the papal role and impact, one can well wonder whether it is possible to have simply a scholarly theological opinion once one is pope. As Benedict XVI, however, he inevitably not just happens to be – as one commentator has put it – 'the leader of [the] largest organized group of followers [of the proclaimed Son of God], the Catholic Church' and as such a highly 'intimidating author' on the subject, but also one invested with an authority denied to other doctrinal specialists in the Catholic Church and outside it. This in itself makes writing such a book an ambiguous event. Starting in the middle of the nineteenth century, the magisterium of the Church changed from a pastoral office for solving conflicts on doctrine to an office for developing an authoritative doctrinal system supposedly expressing the fullness of Catholicism. We may hope it is unintentional, but Ratzinger's book symbolizes the danger of personalizing the magisterium even further, making the specific and personal theology of Joseph Ratzinger the work of the pontiff, thus at least suggesting that it is a normative expression of the Catholic faith.[3]

But it is not only the rather strong criticism of recent developments in christology in Ratzinger's book that makes one wonder whether it is possible to discover something new in christology. The ultimate and returning point of Ratzinger's theology is that Jesus Christ himself is the ultimate and only content of his message. The belief that he is the saviour of the world bears, according to Ratzinger, not much relation to what we spontaneously hope and fear for ourselves, our loved ones, our other fellow human beings and our world. Although the Sermon on the Mount talks about poverty and richness, and about justice and injustice, its message has, in Ratzinger's view, surprisingly little to do with the struggle for justice in which we are already involved and which is to an important degree our context. The message of the Sermon on the Mount is for Ratzinger that Jesus embodies in himself everything that is ultimately good and salvific. Whoever seeks salvation and the fullness of life should turn exclusively to him by turning to the Catholic Church as his sole true representative. This really is a major shift away from many recent attempts to understand Jesus as a historical figure, related to us as historical human beings and thus representing a salvific message.

I cannot but consider it highly significant that Ratzinger's *Jesus of Nazareth* was published shortly after the publication of the official notification on the christology of Jon Sobrino. One of Sobrino's fundamental points is that the exegetical and theological turn to the 'historical Jesus' helps us to realize that we are ultimately saved by the historical Jesus. It is not because Jesus embodied an abstract divine presence and power that we call him saviour and liberator, but because Jesus fully shared the history in which we humans live and have to find our way toward life, justice, and salvation. Jesus opened a way toward salvation and liberation precisely in and related to this history, which was possible because he himself was part of this history.[4] Turning from the 'what' of the message of Jesus' life and preaching, to the 'that' of God's saving presence in it and in him, as Ratzinger does, empties our human history of religious significance and theological meaning. The changes we go through and the discoveries we make in our lives, quite often through severe collective and personal struggles, deep existential crises, and rigid intellectual labour are ultimately without significance in this view, because the problems we are confronted with should not be considered as real problems. Turning to Jesus as God's presence kept alive by the Church is seen as a turning away from these problems. This, in Ratzinger's view, is as it should be, because Jesus' Kingdom is not of this world (cf. John 18: 36). That it is possible for people to behave in this world in such a way that they are participating in God's Kingdom 'that is prepared for them from the foundation of the world' (cf. Matt. 25.34), is far less clear in Ratzinger's book.

II. New Insights

In his book on the future of christology, Roger Haight writes, on the mean-ing of Jesus' suffering and death: 'The cruel torture of Jesus cannot be turned into a good or made into something positive . . . suffering and death in themselves cannot be transformed into a good. I take this as a kind of "bottom line" criterion by which to test a theology of the cross and the language of piety and prayer used by the church to channel devotion.'[5]

I totally agree, but theology has discovered this fairly recently. Haight's statement does not express a sensitivity that has ruled the Christian tradition from the beginning. It is not so clear whether the expressions in the New Testament like 'was it not necessary that the Christ suffered all those things to enter into his glory' (Luke 24.26), or the idea that we are ransomed by the blood of Christ from the futile ways inherited by our forbears (cf. 1 Pet. 1.18–19) does not mean that pain and suffering are sacrifices that are good in themselves, although it is clear that Anselm's view on Jesus suffering as atonement for God's justified rage against the humiliation our sinful exis-tence means to God is not in the New Testament as such.

Our new sensitivity to the danger of calling the evil of suffering good did not come from a revolutionary re-reading of the New Testament either. It comes from the recent history of Christians, theirs and others' experiences of suffering and the traumas that come with it as radical evil. And what is evil in itself cannot have any positive meaning to God or something by which God is pleased. It was during the 1960s and 1970s that criticism of the idea that suffering – and patiently bearing suffering – should be good gained momentum. This idea prolonged suffering and hindered the struggle for the good life that is God's will for all human beings. This made theologians critically re-read their own traditions, including the Bible itself, struggling for an interpretation of the Christian faith that accorded with the recent discovery that the appropriate answer to suffering was to fight it, not to embrace it, but which also had room for the New Testament confessions that the fact that God's Christ had shared our suffering had salvific meaning. For me, it resulted in arguing that the 'necessity' of Christ's suffering lies in the necessity to radically share our fate, including senselessness, exclusion, suffering, and death, to make it possible to be our true and full redeemer. It is not the suffering and death that are good in themselves. They witness to the radical and unreserved will to participate in our humanity – and thus they express a gracious 'self-gift' of the Christ, as is expressed at the Last Supper and repeated in the eucharistic prayer – but are as such a starting point of God's new initiative to save and redeem. We are redeemed by the victory of life in the resurrection, in which we share because the Risen One shared our existence unto death.[6] Since then we live a new, redeemed life.

What it means to lead a certain kind of life can only be found out by leading this life and by analyzing this life. What it means to lead a redeemed life 'in Christ', and thus what it means that Christ is our redeemer, can only be found by describing and analyzing the redemption we live, which includes the fact that our redemption is not fully realized yet. It is in the midst of a world still lying in evil that Jesus Christ as the Word of God made it possible for us to live as children of God (John 1.12). Therefore, it is highly significant that according to Ratzinger the message of Jesus is that he is God's redemptive presence, and just that. The *what* – what this means, how exactly this changes the life of the world and the lives of the people who believe this – is secondary to the *that* of Jesus Christ as the ultimate and unique redeemer of humankind: that is the message throughout the whole of Ratzinger's book on Jesus. This is not just a preference for a Johannine view on Jesus over the Synoptic view, as is often suggested. In the contemporary situation stressing that Jesus is the content of his own message preaches that only the Church as treasurer of this message and as the sacramental representation of his presence connects one to the divine redemption. Believing in Jesus here is not, as in recent christologies, belief in him as the icon of God's coming kingdom of justice, or of God's hidden presence in the poor, the weak, and the excluded, or in hope as resistance against despair. Believing in Jesus means believing in the Roman Catholic Church as the only true entrance to a redeemed existence. This runs through Ratzinger's theology for quite a while now: the Church is the only enclave in which people can be saved from the destructive forces of the world, in fact the destructive forces of modernity.[7]

III. Redemption of the world or redemption from the world?

For someone seeing redemption as redemption from the modern world, as Joseph Ratzinger does, it is hard not to see influence on theology from contemporary thought as polluting its purity. It is almost impossible to see certain developments in the world as what the pastoral constitution on the Church in the Modern World of Vatican II, *Gaudium et Spes,* calls 'signs of the times' (no. 4), places or developments in which God's redeeming presence to the world becomes present to us and makes itself known. This implies that it is extremely difficult really to take into account what I consider to be the major breakthrough of Vatican II: its ability to see the world as the space of God's presence and the Church as the people who see this presence in the midst of the contemporary situation and let themselves be called and gathered by this presence. In the view presented in *Gaudium et Spes,* following Marie-Dominique Chenu, the redeeming God presented and represented by Jesus has to be discovered ever anew, making himself known in the world in ever new, unexpected ways as the 'One Who Is and Will Be'. To know God is to know our ongoing, ever new history.[8] As for Ratzinger, to know the God of Jesus is to stick to the one true message of the Church, free from the contemporary world and always the same, the only true factor of stability and continuity in a rapidly changing world witnessing to a 'dictatorship of relativism'. Against which the Church has to take a stand and to be a dam.[9]

I agree that a certain kind of relativism – there is also a true Christian relativism, as Felix Wilfred argued in this journal[10] – is a thread in Modernity and carries with it a false odium of tolerance, respect, and freedom. But what exactly is the basis for the resistance against relativism? In Ratzinger's case this seems to be the very fact that the Church, basing itself on Jesus' message that as the Son of God he himself presents the absolute, decrees certain values to be absolute. This suggests that these values left to themselves are relative, being made absolute by the preaching of the Church. Is this really as anti-relativist as is suggested? Major christological studies after Vatican II, probably beginning with Edward Schillebeeckx's *Jesus: An Experiment in Christology* and Hans Küng's *On Being a Christian*, both published in 1974, tried to show how in the fully human history of Jesus something came to light that is in itself absolute and has to be endorsed in view of the salvation of humankind. This seems really anti-relativistic to me, witnessing to a belief in the non-relativity of the hidden but truly salfivic presence in God's creation and God's history of salvation.

Granted, the shift toward the historical Jesus in christology after Vatican II has been somewhat confusing. It almost inevitably seemed an attempt to find a historical foundation to the claim that Jesus of Nazareth is Christ, God's Anointed One. What theologians were in fact doing, following the historians and biblical scholars of the so-called Second Quest for the historical Jesus, was analyzing what it means when Christians confess Jesus as their saviour, redeemer, and liberator. In what sense can it be said that he redeemed us? What does it mean to say that he represents God's divine power, being at the same time someone utterly powerless against the massive destructive forces of history? The question was not – although at times it was hard to avoid thinking that it was – what we, as modern people, can still reasonably believe about Jesus, given the level of historical knowledge. The question was how to think God's saving presence in Jesus among us, and therefore, for instance, what Jesus' proclamation of the Kingdom of God really meant. And how – not the least important question –we can still consider this Jesus as our redeemer and liberator, although he lived 2000 years ago. Hence Rahner's reflections on what is means to be a historical human being in need of liberation; hence Jon Sobrino's stress on Jesus' sharing of our historical and always threatened humanity as a precondition of his liberating significance for us; hence Edward Schillebeeckx's development of a theology of grace and its hidden but real presence in the contemporary, secularized world in the second volume of his Christological trilogy.[11]

In effect, the history of Jesus and the history of his disciples with Jesus was presented as the beginning of a new history of which we, 2000 years later, are still part. Elisabeth Schüssler Fiorenza has clearly seen and shown how the New Testament stories about Jesus are told from and telling about the new, redeemed community he made possible. So Christology is not solely about Jesus, but about us in the light of the history of Jesus, and about Jesus as revealed in the salvific effects his words and deeds had and have for human beings.[12] If Jesus is Christ, he does not first have an identity which is then revealed to people, but what he means to people and opens up for them in liberating possibilities is his identity. This in analogy to God, who is who he will be in redeeming and sustaining his people, according to Exodus 3.

IV. New questions

When the Dutch translation of Ratzinger's 2006 book on Jesus of Nazareth was published, I received a phone call from an elderly Catholic who had apparently found my number through the website of the university. He asked me why Ratzinger did not discuss the books of Küng, Schillebeeckx and Schüssler Fiorenza. He found this insulting, after all they had done. I explained to him that I thought that for Ratzinger these theologians were on the wrong track and that he wanted to present a correction. I also tried to explain that I did not agree with Ratzinger and thought that he did not really understand what they were up to, in their christological projects. They, just as he, were trying to explain why we still can and should consider Jesus the embodiment of God's saving power among us. It could be argued, I think, that quite a few times they succeeded better in doing this than he.

However, we should also see that the developments I have sketched extremely briefly in this article lead to new and difficult theological questions. I can mention only two major ones. If our history of understanding him and living as his disciples is part of Jesus' identity, this first of all means that we do not yet know what Jesus' identity as Christ is. Not because we have to do more research, historical, theological, and otherwise, although that is also the case, but fundamentally because our history in the liberating space he opened for us is not finished yet. In the language of the Gospels, we learn new things about Jesus every time we meet him in Galilee, as he has promised (cf. Mark 16.7; Matt. 28.8) – Galilee being the place where we live our common and our individual histories: our struggles with evil, our defeats by evil, and our victories over evil. This implies a major change in understanding religious faith. Faith can no longer be seen as holding on to an unchanging, stable and in this sense certain foundation. It should be seen as an ongoing exploration of the space God's liberating faithfulness opens up for us, individually and collectively. Second, thinking about Jesus' identity as something present in our understanding of him in our lives as his disciples implies that Jesus' identity is not stable. He cannot just seem, but he really can be different things to different people and different communities, at least as long as our history is such that we are not yet able to unite our different points of vies in one encompassing synthesis.

How is all this related to the classical idea that Jesus is the ultimate and definitive revelation of God in our human history? How is it related to the unity of the Church through time and space? How is it related to the fact that the Christian message endorses certain views on God, but firmly contradicts others? Or to the fact that it sees God in certain places – some of them rather unexpected, like the cross – and sees God's presence there as indicative of his presence elsewhere? These questions are important and not all of them could be answered right now, I think, even if I had sufficient space here. But I also think these are the questions we have to ask and think through theologically, because they come with taking seriously that God in and through Jesus shared and shares our history. To try and escape these questions by stressing traditional formulae to me is impossible. It ultimately means refusing the liberty to which we are liberated.

Notes

1. Joseph Ratzinger / Benedict XVI, *Jesus of Nazareth; from the Baptism in the Jordan to the Transfiguration*, New York: Doubleday, 2007 (original ed. 2006).

2. Cf. the documents against the work of Jon Sobrino (2006), Roger Haight (2004), Jacques Dupuis (2001), and the doctrinal declaration *Dominus Jesus* (2000); see http://www.vatican.va/roman_curia/congregations/cfaith/doc_doc_index.htm.

3. Which is, I would argue, highly problematic in principle, because no single person can comprehend and express the fullness of the truth Jesus Christ reveals and represents to us. In a sense, therefore, Ratzinger's accentuation of the personal nature of his book on Jesus is an improvement over pope John Paul II's *Theology of the Body: Human Life in the Divine Plan*, Boston: Pauline Books and Media, 1997, which is also highly personal and sometimes almost idiosyncratic, but is presented as the work of the pope and therefore an integral part of normative Catholic teaching.

4. See especially Jon Sobrino, *Christology at the Crossroads: A Latin American Approach*, London and Maryknoll, NY: SCM Press and Orbis Books, 1978 (1976); *idem, Jesus the Liberator: A Historical-Theological Reading of Jesus of Nazareth*, Tunbridge Wells and Maryknoll, NY: Burns & Oates and Orbis Books, 1993 (1991).

5. Roger Haight, *The Future of Christology*, New York and London: Continuum, 2005, p. 87.

6. I learned this from Edward Schillebeeckx, *Jesus: An Experiment in Christology*, New York: Seabury, 1979 (1974); *idem, Christ: The Experience Of Jesus As Lord*, New York: Crossroad, 1981 (1977).

7. Cf. already my 'On J. Ratzinger, *Principles of Catholic theology*', *The Journal of Religion* 69 (1989), 432–433; being a review of the English translation of Ratzinger's *Theologische Prinzipienlehre. Bausteine zur Fundamentaltheologie*, Munich: Wewel, 1982

8. Cf. my 'Truth as a Religious Concept', *Concilium* 2006/1, 76–85; *idem*, 'The Rediscovery of Truth as a Religious Category: The Enduring Legacy of the Second Vatican Council', *Bulletin ET* 17 (2006) no. 2, 53–56.

9. As is well known, Ratzinger used the phrase 'dictatorship of relativism' in his homily as Dean of the College of Cardinals in the Mass at the beginning of the Conclave after the death of Pope John Paul II on 18 April 2005: 'We are building a dictatorship of relativism that does not recognize anything as definitive and whose ultimate goal consists solely of one's own ego and desires. We, however, have a different goal: the Son of God, the true man. He is the measure of true humanism.' This speech probably got him elected as the new pope.

10. F. Wilfred, 'In Praise of Christian Relativism', *Concilium* 2006/1, 86–94.

11. K. Rahner, *Grundkurs des Glaubens: Einführung in den Begriff des Christentums*, Freiburg: Herder, 1977; Sobrino, *Christology at the Crossroads, loc.cit.*; *idem, Jesus the Liberator, loc. cit.*; Schillebeeckx, *Christ, loc. cit.*.

12. Cf. still E. Schüssler Fiorenza, *In Memory of Her: A Feminist Theological Reconstruction of Christian Origins*, Boston and London: Beacon Press and SCM Press, 1984. Although some of her later works are more theological in the strict sense, it is in the historical studies of *In Memory of Her* that in my view this theological point is made most convincingly.

Masculinity, Femininity, and the Christ

MARIA CLARA LUCCHETTI BINGEMER

Among the various facets of theology that are seeking fresh expression on the basis of the gender perspective, christology is perhaps one of the most important and certainly one of the most polemical. The reason for this is that, while on the one hand Jesus Christ is the central focus of Christian faith and theology, the point of convergence and of our – men's and women's – possibility of accessing the salvation offered by the living God and so the fullness of life this God represents, on the other, many women find that the masculinity of Jesus – the historical-theological fact, that is, that the God of all glory and majesty became incarnate in the person of a male in Palestine 2000 years ago – is not without its problems.

In this article I propose to reflect on this question and the christological challenge it poses, starting with the thinking some major recent feminist theologians have devoted to it. Next, I turn my attention to the Gospels, seeking to discover how Jesus' relations with women are described there and the significance of this attitude in a markedly patriarchal society such as his. Then, I shall seek to reflect theologically on the biblical data considered in tandem with psychology, which questions the separation and firm differentiation between the masculine and the feminine in human persons. Finally, I try to examine the data in a Trinitarian setting, in fidelity to the principle that should guide all Christian theological reflection.

I. Jesus: the man from Nazareth and theological feminism

Many feminist theologians, endeavouring to ponder on revealed mystery from their standpoint of human beings of the feminine gender, find an obstacle in the person and mystery of Jesus Christ.[1] The centrality and lordship of this masculine God strikes them as having been employed – doctrinally, politically, psychologically, and structurally – in the service of a fellowship of brothers and fathers, the Church, whose female members were always counted as auxiliaries or underlings or, in special cases, as so like men so that they could be relatively easily accepted into their company.[2]

The main thrust of feminist critique, nevertheless, does not cover the use made of masculine images to describe God. These, in themselves, can serve as finite points of reference pointing in the direction of God. The problem lies rather in the fact of these images being understood in a literal sense, identifying the mystery with a He, a masculine being. Besides this, there is the problem of utilizing masculine images modelled on a patriarchal outlook. The feminine dimension is simply incorporated artificially into an overall symbol that remains firmly masculine.[3]

Christology has also been viewed by many women as the doctrine in Christian tradition that has most often been used against them. Some statements by great theological masters such as Augustine of Hippo and, in the high Scholastic era, Thomas Aquinas, have been interpreted as saying that the male is the generic sex of the human species. The male alone represents the fullness of human potential, in himself and as head of the woman. He is the totality of the image of God, while woman in herself does not represent the image of God or possess the fullness of humanity.[4]

If Christianity is basically following *of* and identification *with* Jesus Christ; if this constitutes salvation and the full realization of the longings of the human heart, how can women find their place in it, in full faithfulness to their feminine condition? How do they find the way to feeling themselves to be full citizens of the Kingdom put forward by Jesus? How do they find their space in the Revelation of a God with masculine characteristics and in a community made up of his followers that is structured and patterned on essentially male lines?

Although the Church has always proclaimed that the incarnation of God in Jesus Christ is the Good News of Salvation for all: Jews and Greeks, slaves and free, men and women (cf. Gal. 3.28), at all times and in all places, we still find that in most cases the practice does not live up to the pronouncement. All down the ages, women have suffered real and serious discrimination in the church community, not only at the ministerial level but also and above all at the theological level. I believe, nevertheless, that women's theological view of the saving events of the New Testament can uncover new aspects, which, investigated and worked out from a feminine perspective, can provide us with a better basis for stating that christology has an irreplaceable word to speak in the process of liberating women here and now. The key to overcoming this difficulty is to be found, in my view, in a re-encounter with the Jesus of the Gospels, seeking to perceive and contemplate the features of his personality and the steps of his journey just as the first witnesses did. The outcome of such an observation will be discovery of a man who displayed a special kinship and empathy for the women of his time, who founded a community and inaugurated a style of life in which they were welcomed and found their place. A man who, furthermore, showed a deep and harmonious integration between his '*animus*' and his '*anima*', between the masculine and the feminine components of his personality.[5]

II. Considering Jesus . . .

What we can learn about Jesus of Nazareth from the gospel narratives shows him to have been the initiator of an itinerant charismatic group, to which men and women were admitted in a relationship of fraternal friendship. Unlike John the Baptist's movement, which laid marked stress on ascesis and penance, and unlike the Qumran sect, which admitted men only, the movement Jesus inaugurated was characterized – besides its central pre-occupation with preaching the Kingdom as a real project in history – by joy, by sharing without preconditions in celebrations and meals to which sinners and marginal groups in general were admitted, and by the break from a number of taboos associated with the society of his time.

Among these differences, one of the most obvious is that involving relations with women.[6] Any woman of Jesus' time was considered socially and religiously inferior, 'first for not being circumcised and, as a result, not belonging fully to the Alliance with God; then on account of the rigorous purification precepts to which she was obliged because of her biological condition as a woman; and finally because she personified Eve, with all the pejorative charge attached to her.'[8]

The triple Judaic prayer that characterized Rabbinism of the second century came to reflect the mentality predominant in Judaism since Jesus' time – a prayer in which pious Jews gave thanks to God every day for three things: for not having been born a gentile, outside the Law, or a woman.[8] In this context, Jesus' actions proved not merely innovative, but also shocking. Despite not having left any formal teaching on the subject, Jesus' attitude to women was so unheard-of that it surprised the disciples themselves (John 4.27).

The fact that women formed part of the assembly of the Kingdom summoned by Jesus is common to all four Gospels: in this assembly they were not simply accidental components but active and participatory (cf. Luke 10.38–42) and also privileged beneficiaries of his miracles (cf. Luke 8.2; Mark 1.29–31; 5.25–34; 7.24–30, etc.).[9]

This enhancement of women on Jesus' part has a double theological import for us today:

(1) It applies to a particular aspect of the gospel that shows it in its most essential form: the Good News proclaimed to the poor, freed by Jesus as a priority, the deserted, the rejected, pagans, sinners, and those suffering any manner of exclusion, among which women and children were grouped, not being counted as part of Jewish society. Jesus made all these the privileged recipients of his Kingdom, making them fully part of the community of children of God, because his divine vision, constantly informed by the impulses of the Spirit and by his filial relationship with the Father, enabled him to discern hidden values in all these poor, including women: 'the precious life of the trampled reed or the smouldering fire in the still-smoking embers'.[10]

Women played a major role in this evangelical vision of social reversal implied in Jesus' actions and words. It is the women who, among the various categories of the socially excluded, appear as the representatives of the little people and the oppressed. The first talk and recognition of Jesus as Messiah comes from a Samaritan woman (cf. John 4). It is a Syro-Phoenician (cf. Mark 7.24–30) or Canaanite woman (Matt. 15.21–8) who makes Jesus carry out the prophetic gesture of proclaiming the Good News to the gentiles. Among the poor, whom Jesus calls blessed because they are capable of generosity in the midst of deepest need, the figure of the widow (Luke 21.3) stands out as the most destitute and most generous. Prostitutes are singled out as those most marginalized and beyond the law, who will nevertheless be among the first to enter the Kingdom of God (see Mark 21.31). Among the impure, denied access to religious rites and the whole structure of organized religion, the woman with a haemorrhage (Luke 8.4; Matt. 9.20–2) is the prototype, permanently impure according to Jewish law (cf. Lev. 15.19) and rendering everything she touches impure.

Women are, then, a formative and principal part of Jesus' messianic vision and mission, and in it they appear as the most oppressed among the oppressed.[11] They are the lowest step on the social ladder, and are therefore seen as the last who will be first in the Kingdom of God. The burden on their shoulders is the double one of social and cultural, then classist and sexist, oppression. This makes them the favoured recipients of Jesus' liberating proclamation and praxis. This is also why the response of these sufferers from oppression and discrimination to the messianic message is so rapid and so radical. Because they were at the bottom of the heap of social relationships at the time, women were the ones who had most reason and were best placed to long and struggle for the non-perpetuation of the 'status quo' that oppressed and enslaved them.

Jesus' relationship with women carries another component that, closely linked to the first, enriches and complements the picture of the liberating promise of the Kingdom. This is his relationship with women's bodies, a central aspect and the cause of the discrimination to which they were subjected.[12]

With his liberating praxis in relation to women, accepting them just as they are, even with their bodies that were regarded as imperfect and impure in his culture, Jesus proclaimed an integral anthropology, valuing human beings in their dimension of bodies enlivened by the divine breath, as a whole in which spirit and corporeality form a single entity.

As women's biological make-up was, in the society of that time, the central point through which the exclusion to which they were subjected as persons passed, Jesus' actions as shown in the Gospels were definitely and specifically liberating and saving, opening up possibilities and new horizons of communion to all whose whom society excluded and proclaiming the advent of a new humanity in which the original image created by God – 'male and female' (Gen. 1.27) – could be raised to its full stature (cf. Eph. 4.13).

The Gospels, then, do not present a dualism in which masculine and feminine are opposed, in conflict with one another, or even romantic 'complements' to one another. They rather put forward a view of life in which the half of the human race that is still despised and discriminated against has the right of access to a human and egalitarian relationship, one that is adult and responsible. At the same time as preaching this integrated and integrating anthropology, Jesus demonstrates it in his own person and the way he lives his life.

Having looked at Jesus' attitude toward the feminine, we now need to turn our attention to the feminine in Jesus, to the presence of the feminine dimension that Jesus, as the human being he was, bore within himself. The insight of modern psychology – that every human being is, to varying degrees, at once *animus* and *anima*, masculine and feminine – gives us an opening on this point.[13] If this – accepted today as an uncontroversial part of contemporary culture – is true, then Jesus, a man in whom the masculine mode of being a person predominated, also included the feminine dimension in his constitution. Moving beyond the androcentrism of his time, 'he incorporated within himself so many behavioural characteristics that he can be considered the first person to achieve a complete maturity'.[14] The Gospels show us Jesus as a man who did not display the widespread masculine 'shame' at expressing his feelings. Just as he was capable of severely reproaching the Pharisees and his disciples, so he let his lips sing to the Father with joy and thanksgiving when asserting the revelation made to the little ones and hidden from the wise (Matt. 11.25–7); he did not restrain the overflowing tenderness that seized him at the sight of 'harassed and helpless' creatures disregarded by the society of his time (see Mark 9.36 and par.). Furthermore: Jesus experienced in his own person, in the very depth of his being, the emotions and sorrows that afflicted the *'rahamim'* (maternal bowels) of Yahweh in the Old Testament.[15] This can be seen when he weeps at the death of his friend Lazarus (John 11.35) and at the suffering of his beloved Mary of Bethany (John 11.33); when he delivers a bitter and heart-felt lament over the city that will be responsible for his martyrdom (Luke 19.41); when he cries 'woe' to cities that would not accept salvation (Matt. 11.21), and in his cry of frustrated maternal desire to gather the unwilling 'brood' of Jerusalem 'under [his] wings' (Luke 13.34).[16]

III. Jesus, Son of God, human like us in all things . . .

All this feminine nature in Jesus, made up of infinite tenderness, compassion, and mercy, of a delicacy that is not opposed to firmness, of a love that displays longings, gestures, and expressions that can be identified not just as paternal but as maternal as well, and fraternal in a fellowship that is no less a 'sorority', was taken up eternally, definitively, hypostatically, by the Word: that is, by the Second Person of the Trinity.

If we declare that, in Jesus, God becomes 'like us in all things but sin', we are thereby stating that, like any one of us, God lives that inner composition in which the predominance of one aspect of sexuality does not exclude the presence of the other. In Jesus, human, a man from Nazareth, the feminine is really and truly present. On the basis of this affirmation we can, then, go on to say that if God raised him and made him Lord and Christ, his whole personal identity, with all it contained, was divinely assumed. In the life, words, actions, and person of Jesus, the feminine is – finally – divinized in the deepest aspects of his being and so belongs to the innermost nucleus of the mystery of God's love.

Starting with Jesus' resurrection, the Spirit is poured out on all flesh, forming a new humanity, which is none other than the body of Christ. It is this body of Christ, a new creation, collective and all-embracing, that the Spirit continues to form and bring to birth 'groaning in labour pains' (cf. Rom. 8.22–3) until now, making the original image of the Father's creation – a creation that is 'male and female' (Gen. 1.27) – present in the world. And this creation finds its prototype in Christ, the first-born of all creatures.[17] In this christology, women are not only announcers of the Risen Christ but also identified with his actual person. Women too speak, live, and act, in a very deep sense, '*in persona Christi*'. They too are an '*alter Christus*'.[18]

The early Church assimilated all this in a profound and creative fashion. The New Testament contains many examples of prophetesses (Acts 19.8–9) and deaconesses (Rom. 16.1). Later the Church of the catacombs and martyrs of the first three centuries, in its turn, witnessed innumerable women – like men – shedding their blood for their faith in Jesus Christ, the embodiment of the dead and raised Lord.[19]

This christology of the early centuries, developed under the powerful impact of experience of the Spirit and marked by eschatological expectation of the coming *parousia*, made no distinction between the past history of Jesus of Nazareth and the present time of the risen Christ. Nor did it separate these from the pre-existence of the Word that antedates creation. In it, Jesus Christ is the one who continues to reveal himself in persons – men and women – in an ever-expanding potential for a new humanity. The reality of Jesus Christ was not completed or closed off in the earthly life of Jesus but continued being present in the body of the risen Lord, made up of all those men and women who gave their lives, in one way or another, for the coming of the Kingdom.

We should not forget, however, that in this risen but still crucified Lord, rather than crucified then risen, creation re-acquires its original light. Made reality in Christ – the first-born of all creatures – the image of the divine community – Father, Son, and Holy Spirit – is made present in the world in the human community – men and women. The Christ who is the prototype of humanity is – also and equally – the prototype of women. The Second Person of the Trinity –the Word made flesh – is salvation for women too.

Women, victims of the dual social and religious oppression at the historical moment the Word became flesh, are, together with other outcasts awaiting Jesus' call, privileged representatives of a new social order in which the will of God will be made known and will fill the earth. Jesus Christ, who on the one hand cannot simply be reduced to the spatio-temporal dimensions of the man from Nazareth but at the same time has to be proclaimed and venerated as *Kyrios* (glorified and glorious Lord), cannot, on the other hand, be confined by christology to the glorious lordship of the Risen Lord, forgetting that he who reigns at the Father's right hand is the same person who washed his disciples' feet, who showed himself as the servant who gave his life for his friends, obedient even unto death on a cross. He is the one who showed preference for the poor and oppressed, identifying himself as one of them. And he is the same person who treated the despised and downtrodden women of his time with affection and respect, proclaiming their full dignity as daughters of God and citizens of the Kingdom.

Conclusion: the two faces of the mystery of Jesus Christ

The glory of the resurrection is nothing other than the seal of approval given to the historical path taken by this Jesus – servant and brother – as the only path that leads to salvation. To forget this is to remove oneself from the centre of the New Testament *kerygma* and so from faith in Christ itself.

The Christian community, made up of men and women, gives continuity to this all-embracing Christ, bringing about – with the assistance of the Holy Spirit – the full liberation of the cosmos and of humankind. Christology is thus still today – as ever and never more so than now – Good News of salvation for women seeking their space and their place, side-by-side with men, in society and in the Church.

In the Son, God became flesh of men and women. The Son of the Father, pre-existing from all eternity and who gave us the power to be children of God and to call this God Father, is also the son of Mary (cf. Mark 6.3; Matt. 13.55; John 6.42), born of woman (cf. Gal. 2.4). This is the process of kenotic descent celebrated in the Letter to the Philippians (2.5–8). The one in whom we believe as risen and glorious is in no wise different from the child who was born of Mary's flesh and from this Galilean woman received the body of God walking the ways of humanity's land. Having come from the womb of that young woman from Nazareth, he would grow in grace and wisdom and surprise his contemporaries, who, seeing the signs and wonders he performed, would say, 'Is not this the carpenter's son? Is not his mother called Mary?' (Matt. 13.55; cf. Mark 6.3; John 6.42).

At the centre of the mystery of the incarnation, a mystery that is salvation for the whole human race, the New Testament places man and woman, Jesus and Mary, God who takes human flesh *in* and *through* the flesh of the woman – 'born of woman'. God does not become man and identify himself with just one half of humankind; God becomes flesh, flesh of man and woman, in such a manner that the way to the Father must necessarily lead through the overall human condition, which is masculine and feminine.

The mystery of the incarnation of Jesus in the flesh of Mary teaches us that human beings are not divided into a body of sin and imperfection and a spirit of greatness and transcendence. It is only in the weakness, poverty, and limitations of human flesh – flesh of men and women – that the ineffable greatness of the Spirit can be experienced, contemplated, and adored. And it is only here that theology can, finally, stammer its word.

Translated by Paul Burns

Notes

1. The most balanced critiques are, among US women theologians, in works such as E. Johnson, *She Who Is: The Mystery of God in Feminist Theological Discourse*, New York: Crossroad, 1992, and, among Europeans, K. E. Börresen, *Subordination and Experience: the nature and role of woman in Augustine and Thomas Aquinas*, London: SCM Press, 1968; *idem* (ed.) *Image of God and Gender Models in Judaeo-Christian Tradition*, Minneapolis, MN: Fortress, 1995. The most radical must include Mary Daly, whose *Beyond God the Father* (Boston: Beacon Press, 1973) became a sort of manifesto for the dawning feminist theology.

2. Cf. the question of the eternal feminine, so much criticized by feminism. On this see *Concilium* 2000/5, *In the Power of Wisdom*, especially the Editorial by E. Schüssler Fiorenza, 'Walking in the Way of Wisdom', pp. 7–10.

3. E. Schüssler Fiorenza, *Jesus, Miriam's Child. Critical Issues in Feminist Theology*, New York: Crossroad, 1994; E. Johnson, 'The Maleness of Christ', *Concilium* 1991/6, *The Special Nature of Women?*, pp. 108–16; *idem, She Who Is, op. cit.; idem., Consider Jesus: Waves of Renewal in Christology*, New York: Crossroad, 2001.

4. See, e.g., the commentary by R. Radford Ruether in *To Change the World: Christology and Cultural Criticism*, New York: Crossroad, 1983, p. 45. See also Börresen, *Subordination and Experience, op. cit.*

5. Cf. the excellent article by R. M. Ceballos, 'La masculinidad patriarcal y la masculinidad liberadora. El modelo de Jesús de Nazaret', *Anuario Pedagógico* 11 (Santo Domingo: Centro Cultural Poveda, 2007). In this he distinguishes the

masculinity of Jesus from traditional patriarchal masculinity and argues that Jesus represents the true destiny of the male, in a liberating masculinity.

6. Cf. www.pucsp.br/rv2_2005/p_kochmann.pd44 (accessed 6 Apr. 2008) and what R. S. Kochmann says on the place of women in Judaism through history.

7. L. Boff, *O rosto materno de Deus*, Petrópolis: Vozes, 1979, pp. 77–8. See also my article '"*Chiarete*. Alegrai-vos" (Lc 15.8–10) ou a mulher não futuro da Teologia da Libertação', REB 48 (1988), 565–87.

8. Cf. R. S. Kochmann's words in the text cited above, n. 5, at p. 36.

9. See Boff, *O rosto materno, op.cit.*; A. M. Tepedino, *As discípulas de Jesus*, Petrópolis: Vozes, 1990; C. Ricci, *Mary Magdalen and Many Others: Women who followed Jesus*, Tunbridge Wells: Burns& Oates, 1993; M. C. L. Bingemer, *O segredo feminino do Mistério*, Petrópolis: Vozes, 1991; M. P. Aquino, *Nuestro clamor por la vida. Teología latinoamericana desde la perspective de la mujer*, San José: DEI, 1992, among others.

10. R. Laurentin, 'Jesus and Women: An Underestimated Revolution', *Concilium* 134 (1980), *Women in a Men's Church*, pp. 80–92.

11. Cf. R. Radford Ruether, *Sexism and God-talk*, Boston: Beacon Press, 1993, p. 84.

12. I refer to what I said above on the fact of women being kept apart from public and religious life on account of their biological make-up, which led to them often being considered impure.

13. On this point, see Boff, *op. cit.* pp. 102–3, strongly influenced by C. G. Jung. See also *idem*, *Trinity and Society*, Tunbridge Wells: Burns & Oates and Maryknoll, NY: Orbis Books, 1992.

14. J. Moltmann and E. Moltmann Wendel, *Dieu home et femme*, Paris: C erf, 1984, p. 58.

15. For a fuller consideration of this subject see my 'A Trindade a partir da perspective da mulher', REB 46 (1986), 73–99 (re-worked and extended in ' Abbá: un padre maternal', *Estudios Trinitarios* vol. 36 (2002), pp. 69–102.

16. On this point I refer, *inter alia*, to S. McFague, *Models of God. Theology for an Ecological, Nuclear Age*, Philadelphia: Fortress, 1988; V. Molenkott, *The Divine Feminine. The Biblical Imagery of God as Feminine*, New York: Crossroad, 1987; also Johnson, *She Who Is*.

17. Cf. Börresen, *Image of God and Gender Models, op. cit.* (n. 1 above).

18. These expressions, which in the Catholic Church are reserved to priests, can, I believe, justifiably be applied to all Christians, who, by virtue of their Baptism, are made one with Christ in his paschal mystery. Therefore, such expressions are applicable to women too. Cf. what E. Johnson says on this in 'The Maleness of Christ', *art. cit.*.

19. Cf. the 'Letter from the Churches of Lyon and Vienne' describing the martyrdom of the young Blandina and the slave Felicity, where there are clear com-

parisons and analogies with Christ. Cf. P. Allard, *Histoire des persécutions pendant la première moitié du IIme siècle*, Paris, 1886, p. 73 (cited by L. Bouyer, *Le Consolateur*, Paris: Cerf, 1980, p. 127).

Christological Pluralism: Some Reflections

FELIX WILFRED

I. Apophatic christologies

Plato's allegory of the dark cave in his *Republic*, the Upanishad's approach to Brahman as *neti . . . neti* (not this . . . not this), and Dionysius the Areopagite's negative theology all point to the ineffable character of the Divine and the 'darkness' enveloping it (cf. Ps. 18:11). This apophatic tradition, I think, could profitably be channelled to the understanding of the mystery of Jesus Christ. As the symbol of the Divine, Jesus Christ reveals but in a way also conceals the Divine, so that the quest for the divine mystery through Jesus Christ continues for us in a plurality of ways. Even more, Jesus Christ himself shares in the ineffability of the mystery of the Divine in spite of its historical manifestation and revelation. What he represents in relation to God and to humanity, we only partially understand through the testimony of the scriptures and experiences of encounter with him through the ages.

Totalizing systems of christology do not lead us, as often presumed, to the full mystery of Jesus Christ, who remains *semper maior* (ever greater). Speaking of the love of Christ, Paul turns contemplative and marvels at 'the breadth and length and height and depth' of the love of Jesus Christ which 'surpasses knowledge' (Eph 3:18). This apophatic character and incommensurability call for a multiplicity of christologies, all of which remain dwarfed in the face of the overwhelming mystery with which they deal. All christologies share the same lot; they all have a place, but none of them can claim to be *the* ultimate explanation of Jesus Christ. In other words, any christology has to be, at bottom, necessarily, apophatic. There is enough reason, then, why a plurality of christologies is to be welcomed.

II. Decentralized hermeneutical paths

We understand the significance of this plurality also by following a hermeneutical path according to which the many faces of Jesus can be discovered only when looked at from the perspective of the reader of the text. The text of the New Testament yields multiple interpretations from the experience-horizon of the reader and interpreter. This is something more than trying to retrieve the image of the historical Jesus by the application of historico-critical method. One needs to go beyond a reconstruction of the past and arrive at a plurality of christologies through deployment of *literary-critical hermeneutics* that brings the contextual world of the reader and the text into dialogue and conversation. Christologies resulting from such a hermeneutical process are creative and are attuned to change and transformation. A close study of various contextual christologies of today will confirm this.

The historical Jesus never gave a single picture of himself. Early Christianity lived with an extremely rich variety of christologies, with none of them as *the* norm or model for others. It is striking that within the same Judaism there were different interpretations of Jesus Christ, and in his lifetime Jesus was viewed from different viewpoints – as new Moses, prophet, messiah, Son of God, redeemer, and the like. Even within the life of a single author like Paul, we can find different christologies. One thing is to see a plurality of images of Jesus within the New Testament; another thing is the attempt to collapse them all into one single model, in which case we have to admit that the various christologies contradict each other.

> If, for example, the christologies of Mark and Matthew were taken simply as positive affirmations, pronounced from the same perspective, in non-symbolic language, one could not hold both integrally at the same time. At certain points these christologies contradict each other. But, of course, this is contrary to fact: one can hold all of the New Testament christologies together. This is so precisely because they are symbolic affirmations about transcendent aspects of Jesus Christ, conceived from different perspectives, and not adequately 'containing' their object.[1]

A plurality of christologies was to continue through subsequent centuries, giving birth to new concepts and images.[2] Each christology had its validity as it came up in a particular context and culture and responded to the issues and questions raised in that particular milieu and from horizons of different experiences. Today, very fertile feminist christologies are coming out of women's experience and their reading of the scriptures. We have very innovative African, Asian, and Latin American christologies.[3] They result from a re-reading of the Gospels from a particular location. Understood in a symbolic sense, many contextual christologies today could and do co-exist without them needing to invoke any one single model of the past, or being subjected to any attempt to unify them under one single register.

III. Religious pluralism and christologies

The many christologies of today have to come to terms in one form or other with the reality of religious pluralism. The question today is: Can Jesus Christ be interpreted in such a way that people who have been sustained by their religious traditions – Hinduism, Buddhism, Taoism, etc. – need not break their spiritual journey to encounter Jesus Christ, but can meet him on their spiritual journey and interpret him as they experience him? This could lead to a new realization of the journey already made and project the path yet to be traversed. This appropriation in the world of spiritual quest is indispensable for making sense of the mystery of Jesus Christ in the encounter of religions. We accordingly need to probe into a pluralist understanding of revelation itself.[4]

Ultimately what is at stake in christology is the mystery of the union of the divine and the human. Here too there is a fundamental difference in conceiving the manner of the union, which also colours and qualifies our understanding of the mystery of incarnation. If the divine and the human are not viewed as two distant entities that need to be brought together, but viewed as being much closer to one another, as is for example, the Hindu conception, then the understanding of the manifestation of the divine through incarnation will also differ according to this basic difference in understanding these two realities. In a world-view in which the distance between the divine and human is wide, and the distinction is sharp, the reality of mediation acquires prime importance.

Where the relationship is conceived differently, incarnation as divine manifestation is not viewed as uniting two separate realities, but as bringing together the two realities already united into a much closer union and intimacy. Seen from this perspective, the significance of Jesus Christ is to open our eyes to the nearness and intimacy of God and to awaken us to the divine within. His own mystery is enveloped within this reality of divine and human union and communion. In other words, he makes it possible for us to experience the mystery of God in whom 'we live and move and have our being' (Acts 17:28). This is something different from the concept of mediation (*mesites*) between God and humanity.

The approach to the mystery of Jesus Christ in a religiously pluralist context calls for the abandoning of the ontological moorings. It is not true that the best defence of Christian theology and especially of christology lies in metaphysics. Such a close relationship, unfortunately, has resulted in the de-christianization of the West following the dissolution of metaphysics with no alternatives.[5] There seems to be a certain convergence between the post-metaphysical thought with theologies and christologies inspired by religious pluralism. These christologies keep the mystery of Jesus Christ alive and life-giving without needing any recourse to ontological categories. That leads me to the next point.

IV. Non-Christian christologies

The dominant question hitherto has been how other religions are related to Christ and how Christ is related to other religious traditions. The question needs to be posed differently today from an experiential point of view and with reference to *peoples* of other religious traditions, and not merely from a theoretical perspective. It is more important to know how peoples of other faiths have approached the person and message of Christ in their spiritual journey. This is an empirical and experiential issue which can provide very useful theoretical insights.

We need to be aware of the fact that very often the search for Christ is part of the spiritual quest of our neighbours of other faiths, and even their mysticism. Therefore we need to pay sufficient attention to the way they view Jesus Christ and appropriate his person and message in their lives. This is more important than the question of how Jesus Christ is present in other religious traditions, which has assumptions and presuppositions of the classical christology.

I may say without any exaggeration that the peoples of South Asia, for example, have learned more deeply about Jesus Christ from the way Mohan Roy, Gandhi, and Vivekananda drew ethical implications from his life and teachings, from the faith with which Keshab Chandra Sen interpreted his person, and from the manner the illiterate mystic Ramakrishna experienced him, than from the formula of Chalcedon on the metaphysical essence of

Jesus Christ, which is far removed from their world-view and philosophy. There is in varying degrees a soteriological understanding of Jesus Christ in non-Christian christologies, in as much as he makes present the power of divine salvation viewed in different ways but ultimately contributing to the fullness and integration of the life of the world and of the universe.[6]

It may be argued that non-Christian interpretations of Jesus Christ do not touch upon the Christ of faith. But the fact is that among many non-Christians there is an approach to Jesus that reveals faith in him, since they do not simply seek information about Jesus, but encounter with him and experience of him as part of their spiritual quest. We have in the Gospels the incident of the Greeks wanting 'to see' Jesus (John 12:20). In another incident, the disciples try to stop someone driving out demons in Jesus' name 'because', as they argued, '*he was not following us*' (Mark 9:40). Here is a question of widening a narrowly-defined understanding of discipleship and appreciating the faith of others in following him and invoking his name.

Further, it is not true that faith is at work only when Jesus is viewed as Christ. We could, as early followers did, encounter in faith the Jesus of history, his life and teaching. There is a faith in trying to experience Jesus' message and in attempting to follow his path (*imitatio Christi*). It may be recalled here that Vivekananda, the founder of a Hindu monastic order, not only translated the *Imitation of Christ* by Thomas à Kempis into the Bengali language in 1889 but also prescribed regular reading of it to his monks.

Ultimately, the legitimation of non-Christian christologies derives from the necessary and crucial distinction between the Jesus of history and the Christ of faith. The plan of God, the mystery of the Word, of Christ, and of the action of the Spirit have an inclusive character.[7] The non-Christian interpretations of Jesus have to be placed in this larger horizon. This could be seen in the attitude of many Hindus, for example, who see in Jesus Christ the embodiment of all those ideals Hinduism stands for. And if we admit that religions themselves are sites where the mystery of the plan of God and the Word and the Spirit are at work, then interpretations by non-Christians of Jesus Christ take us into new depths and to reassessment of classical christology. The historical Jesus, let alone the mystery of Christ, is beyond the control of the institutional Church, whose formulations of christology cannot be invoked as criterion or become normative for non-Christian christologies. These christologies are not only legitimate but indispensable for a more complete and deeper understanding of the mystery of Jesus Christ.

When their religious traditions themselves reflect the saving presence of God and the activity of the Spirit, what they say about the mystery of Jesus Christ has to be taken at the level of faith. These christologies are not mere external additions and corollaries, but are to be viewed as expressions of the universality of the mystery of Jesus Christ, which is not the monopoly of baptized Christians. These christologies widen our mental horizons and provide a larger scope, and they consequently also allow us to see more clearly the limitations of the classical christology and the formulations of the Councils.

There is another reason why non-Christian understanding of Jesus Christ is indispensable today. The life, ministry, and teaching of the historical Jesus were centred on the Kingdom of God and the salvation promised by God to the poor. There are, as Aloysius Pieris notes, two categories of poor – 'the poor by circumstances' and the 'poor by choice':

> The majority of the poor summoned by God to be God's covenant partners in the project of liberation are non-Christians! The first category (victims of Mammon, who represent Christ 'as we know him now') constitutes the bulk of the world's population, most of which is concentrated in non-Christian Asia. Included in the second category (renouncers of Mammon, who follow Jesus 'as he was in the days of his flesh') are so many co-agents of liberation, guides in the path of righteousness, discoverers and announcers of the Saving Truth, founders and advocates of Religions. These are not rivals in a conversion race but partners in a common mission. Jesus, in whom the Triune God is covenanted with the poor, needs their collaboration to arrive *with them* at the fullness of Christhood. Jesus cannot be Christ without them.[8]

What has been said leads us to consider more closely the issue of soteriology in relation to christology

V. Pluralism in soteriology

Soteriology is in the very structure of christology. Christological pluralism implies, then, not only different images of Jesus Christ but also different understandings of salvation. In the New Testament it is so evident that Jesus is inextricably linked to salvation from God. However, there is a plurality in the New Testament itself regarding what salvation consists in. It has to do a lot with the questions and issues with which people interpret Jesus Christ against their social, cultural, and historical backgrounds. It is presumptuous, therefore, to think that an understanding of salvation can be inferred *a priori* from the structure of the human spirit, independent of the human embeddedness in a particular history, culture, context, and so forth.

The multiplicity of soteriology resulting from different worlds of experience enriches the understanding of salvation and the mystery of Jesus Christ. The dark night of suffering of the black people, the humiliations of the 'Untouchables' of India, the experience of marginalization by the indigenous peoples, the anguish of the innocent HIV/AIDS patients and the agonies of the terminally ill have found in the experience of Jesus and his life an understanding of salvation that can hardly fit into any classical soteriology of atonement.[9] It would make little sense to these victims to hold that Jesus died *in substitution* for them and their sins, whereas it brings his mystery closer to their life when his life, teachings, sufferings, and death are interpreted as having taken place *in solidarity with them*.

One of the convictions that is gaining ground out of the contextual experiences is that salvation cannot simply be confined to the death of Jesus, but has to be viewed in the light of his entire life, teaching, and approach to the people and to God. The Jesus of history, now encountered as the presence and revelation of God, is saving. It is not so much his death and the blood shed in the past that save, but rather it is the communion with him today, in his identity as crucified and resurrected (cf. Rom. 8:34) and the following of his teachings and life-path that bring about salvation. 'This is indeed the will of my Father, that all who see the Son and believe in him may have eternal life; and I will raise them up on the last day' (John 6:40). In other words, the historical Jesus bears in different ways the saving presence of God, which challenges any metaphysical explication of him as the necessary basis for the understanding of salvation. In fact, the non-Christian christologies we considered earlier bring to our awareness the significance of the historical Jesus and his life and ministry for salvation, something that has been neglected in the traditional soteriology.

VI. The classical christology of the Western Church *vis-à-vis* christological pluralism

In the midst of a plurality of christologies and therein implied soteriologies, how do we view classical christology today? From a historical point of view, it is only since Chalcedon that the institutional Church took refuge in one single christology – which needs to be reviewed today. By no means does the Chalcedonian christology epitomize the New Testament christologies, as often claimed. Chalcedon, in fact, depends on one single strand of New Testament christology, which is related to the pre-existence of Christ, whereas many contextual christologies have other accents deriving inspiration from the same New Testament and its other models. That is why Chalcedon needs to be balanced – not to say corrected – by the plurality of christologies in the New Testament, especially the ascending christologies interpreting the theocentric orientation of Jesus Christ (*eis ton theon*) and his faith.

The Chalcedonian formula of christology has a paradigmatic value today. It is the best classical example of how to maintain orthodoxy in the midst of 'heresies' at a time when the discernment between the two was a crucial matter for the life of the Church, which may not be the case at all periods of history and is certainly not in our times. How could a formulation about Jesus Christ that does not speak of his life, history, teaching, death and resurrection become normative to understanding his mystery? That prompted Pablo Richard to speak of '*Jesus without a face*' in these formulations.[10] Moreover, how could a formulation that is couched in symbolic language – as all religious languages are – be normative for all other symbolic expressions of the mystery of Jesus Christ expressed in other cultural universes?[11]

All human symbols have an inherent ambiguity. This is true of images of Jesus both in classical christology and in modern contextual christologies. For example, one may be alert to the negative and authoritarian connotation involved in viewing Jesus as 'chief' in the African culture. But then, has not the classical notion of Jesus as *kyrios* (Lord) carry the same danger?[12] But in fact, as a classic in christology, Chalcedon cannot represent a closure but a source of inspiration and motivation for innovative christologies in the present-day context.

The claim that one single christology orders all others and assigns value to each one of them cannot but be characterized as a hegemonic theological trend that is destructive of the enriching and inspiring pluralism in christology. In fact, however, even after Nicaea and Chalcedon, which were supposed to put an end to controversies, other christologies continued to flourish.

Christological pluralism is very crucial also today. Pluralism allows the voices of the weaker ones to be heard as they encounter and express the mystery of Jesus Christ in their lives and struggles. If, as is being increasingly realized, the axis of Christianity has shifted to the poorest parts of our world, and the weaker sections of humanity are deeply attached to his person and message, we need to ask them, rather than the classical christology, what makes Jesus Christ so appealing to them in the midst of their poverty. There is no reason why the voices of the poor and their interpretation of Jesus Christ should be sidelined in favour of one single normative model. In fact, endless repetition of Chalcedonian christology has stifled the emergence of new and vibrant christologies, as the history of missions shows, and in many cases has rendered ineffective the cause of evangelization.

The limits of the Chalcedonian formula and of classical christology lie not only in the *absence of any soteriology* and silence on the life, death, passion and resurrection of Christ, but also in the way they reduce the understanding of Christ to the level of the mind, whereas a true understanding and truth of Christ is to be derived from the involvement of the whole person – feeling, emotions, existential questions and issues through which the innumerable christologies of popular religiosity, for example, approach his mystery. These christologies have in fact nourished the life of the Christian communities tom a greater extent than the official christology.

Conclusion: toward contemplative pluralism

There is no single christology that can ever claim to be whole or complete. All christologies are partial and fragmentary.[13] This is not a defect, since we are given to understand the divine mystery in Jesus Christ only in glimpses.

The pluralism as used in the conceptual cluster of 'exclusivism, inclusivism, and pluralism' has become sterile. It does not take us anywhere as it is entangled in endless knots of controversies smacking of nominalism and caught up in a conceptual labyrinth. Moreover, in christology we need a contemplative approach to pluralism rather than a systemic or epistemic one. Epistemic pluralism is operative when plurality is structured into a system, and the differences are viewed but as various expressions of a well-defined unitary concept, doctrine, etc. In this kind of pluralism, various christologies reflecting different horizons of experiences are not given due attention in their *difference* and specificity, but are quickly reduced to a common denominator or common ground. The plurality resulting from the difference of gender, culture, soil, language, and historical spaces are such that they do not permit us to conclude as if the differences are variations of one single concept, or to force them all into the procrustean bed in the name of a common ground. The poor of the world, who are passionately attached to the person and message of Jesus today, bring a plurality of christologies from their world of marginalization.

Contemplative pluralism does not deny the need for unity behind plurality but simply says that the unity is not to be viewed as something already available or given (classical christology, Chalcedonian formula, theocentrism, etc.) but as something hidden and forming the object of our continuous quest that is refreshing and transforming. The understanding of contemplative pluralism goes hand in hand with an apophatic approach to christology.

Apophatic christology and contemplative pluralism create room for and valorize the experiences of our neighbours of other faiths and their christological discourses and interpretations, as well as the struggles of the poor for a fuller life. Apophatic christology is open-ended and does not permit any manipulation. It challenges any attempt to domesticate christology to particular ends, such as upholding patriarchy or justification of any power-agenda within the Christian community. Fostering contemplative pluralism and apophatism remains a great challenge for all christologies.

Notes

1. Roger Haight, *Jesus. Symbol of God*, Maryknoll, NY: Orbis Books, 2002, p. 181; cf also George M. Soares-Prabhu, 'The Jesus of Faith. A Christological Contribution to an Ecumenical Third World Spirituality', in his *Theology of Liberation. An Indian Biblical Perspective*, Pune: Jnana-Deepa Vidyapeeth, 2001, pp. 267–95; Edward Schillebeeckx, *Jesus. An Experiment in Christology*, London: Collins, 1979; Raymond E. Brown, *An Introduction to New Testament Christology*, Mahwah, NJ: Paulist Press, 1994.

2. Cf. Jaroslav Pelikan, *Jesus through the Centuries: His Place in the History of Culture*, New York: Harper & Row, 1987.

3. A detailed study of these various christologies is obviously beyond the scope of this brief article. The literature on these christologies is steadily growing. See for example: M. Amaladoss, *The Asian Jesus*, Delhi: IDCR/ISPCK, 2005; R. Sugirthrajah (ed.), *Asian Faces of Jesus*, Maryknoll, NY: Orbis Books, 1993; Robert Schreiter (ed.), *Faces of Jesus in Africa*, Maryknoll, NY: Orbis Books, 1995; Jon Sobrino, *Jesus in Latin America*, Maryknoll, NY: Orbis Books, 1987; Errol D'Lima and Max Gonsalves (eds), *What Does Jesus Christ Mean? The Meaningfulness of Jesus Christ amid Religious Pluralism in India* (Proceedings of

the 21st Annual Seminar of the Indian Theological Association), Bangalore: The Indian Theological Association, 1999.

4. Cf. Andrés Torres Queiruga, 'Rethinking Pluralism: from Inculturation to "Inreligionation"', *Concilium* 2007/1, pp. 102 – 11.

5. Cf. Gianni Vattimo, *After Christianity*, New York: Columbia University Press, 2002.

6. Cf. M. M. Thomas, *The Acknowledged Christ of the Indian Renaissance*, Madras: C.L.S., Madras, ²1976; Chaturvedi Badrinath, *Finding Jesus in Dharma*, Delhi: ISPCK, 2000; Robin Boyd, *An Introduction to Indian Christian Theology*, Delhi: ISPCK, 2000.

7. If we can still use the category of 'inclusivism', it needs to be qualified. We can speak of a theocentric inclusivism, which means looking at the matter from the perspective of God and God's plan of salvation. Here there is no exclusion. For it includes everyone (cf. I Tim. 2:4–6). However, if inclusivism is understood in a christocentric way, namely whatever is good and holy in other religions belongs to Christ – Christ understood as Christians understand him – then it is a problematic inclusivism.

8. Aloysius Pieris, 'Christ Beyond Dogma. Doing Christology in the Context of the Religions and the Poor' (a paper originally prepared for the Jesuit Ecumenical Congress, Kottayam, India, 1999), p. 18.

9. On the other hand, it should be recognized that the predominant soteriology of Anselm was an attempt to respond to the contextual needs of his times. By employing reasoning in soteriology, he tried to overcome the mythological explanation of redemption and, at the same time, responded to the unbelievers who found incarnation not in conformity with reason. See Hans Kessler, *Die theologische Bedeutung des Todes Jesu. Eine traditionsgeschichtliche Untersuchung*, Düsseldorf: Patmos Verlag, 1970.

10. Cf. Pablo Richard, 'Different Faces of Jesus in the Synoptic Gospels' in *Concilium* 2002/1, pp. 41–8.

11. For many insights on the difference between classical Christology and new christological attempts, see the excellent work of Jon Sobrino, *Christology at the Crossroads*, Maryknoll;, NY: Orbis Books, 1978.

12. Cf. François Kabasélé, 'Christ as Chief', in Robert Schreiter (ed.), *op.cit.* pp. 103 ff.

13. Cf. Felix Wilfred, *Margins: Site of Asian Theologies*, Delhi: ISPCK, 2008, pp. 189ff.

II. DOCUMENTATION/THEOLOGICAL FORUM

Papal Attempts to Gain Authority in the Contemporary World

KARL GABRIEL

I. Introduction

Before investigating the ways in which the present pope seeks to acquire and to stabilize authority, it seems appropriate to examine the worldwide social context in which religions exist and function today. In the first pronouncements of his pontificate, the Pope dealt with specific topics that could not fail to have repercussions for religions in a global context. A proficient analysis of the implications of authority calls for them to be viewed, so it seems, at the point of tension between the typically modern differentiation of the forms of exercise and reception of authority and simultaneous strategies devised and used to counter any such differentiation. We have to ask whether Benedict XVI is not carrying on, though in his own style, the strategies used by John Paul II both to neutralize any differentiation of papal authority and to endow it with a charismatic quality. All this prompts a consideration of the possible consequences with regard to the situation of the Catholic Church, not only within the Church itself but in the context of worldwide society.

II. Papal authority and religion in a universal social context

One of the most conspicuous recent developments of the present-day world is its tendency to perceive religions in a worldwide context, and to allocate them a central role in the global society that is coming into existence.[1] If we stop trying to restrict the concept of society to European national societies, and relate it instead to a global framework, it seems permissible and indeed unavoidable to speak of 'post-secular society'.[2] Throughout the world today religious traditions are seen increasingly in terms of a common reference system for religion or religions. Consequently, the general concept of religion is entering a new phase in its historical development. Whereas at first it helped to articulate what was common to the Christian denominations in spite of their contentions, and in the nineteenth century was shaped by the scientific and scholarly approaches to religion which were emerging then, nowadays it has acquired a new function as a worldwide point of reference and also provides a context in which it is possible to express the common elements of the most varied cultural traditions. The many religions in the world are beginning to form a global system of religion with its own pluralistic structure.[3] Nowadays, when discussing religious leaders, with regard not only to John Paul and Benedict but to the Dalai Lama and other representatives of religious communities, a global religious system is the common point of reference. At present, the dynamics of the system of religons has a three-fold orientation. On the one hand, it is a question of the generalization of what religion in a worldwide context is, or ought to be. On the other hand, difference, the profile of individual religions and the competitiveness of religious communities in a global framework are matters of prime concern. The third orientation has to do with the distinctive nature of religion and its relation to modern secular society and thought, especially to the secular State and to secular science and thought.

This framework of wordwide society is the context in which Benedict XVI seeks to acquire authority. It is possible to distinguish two major topics by means of which the Pope is trying to make sure that he gains authority in this heterogeneous state of the global system of religions.[4] First comes the commitment of all 'true' religions to a unique loving God, who is diametrically opposed to all expropriations and adoptions for violent ends. This is one of the main orientations of the encyclical *Deus caritas est*. A second message concerns the relationship between religion and secular reason. In this connection the Pope puts forward the idea of a reciprocal cleansing. Secularism needs purification by religion in order to be its true self as an authentic secular State. On the other hand, religion should take account of its reflection by secular thought in order to realize its true nature and to detect its blind spots.[5]

The Pope sees this interaction of religion and secularism as the specific profile proper to Christianity with its satisfactory response to the challenge that all religions have to face. At all events, he presumes that the reflective glass of reason has been tarnished on its journey toward the modern world in the West, and that it could really carry out its function only in the pre-modern union of reason and faith. As became especially clear with

Benedict's Regensburg address, in this respect the Pope's claim to authority and to ordain thinking in a worldwide context is contradicted both by Protestant tradition and by Islam, as well as by representatives of contemporary secularism.

III. Structures of authority as a relationship

From the viewpoint of the social sciences, authority is a reciprocal social relationship.[6] Authority is always conferred, too, by those to whom the claims of authority are addressed. It is not the termination of authority that is typical of modern societies, but rather a process of differentiating or distinguishing the authority relationship in very distinct patterns.[7] A primary distinction has to do with the manifold forms of functional authority in relation to formal authority or to official authority in a formal complex or setting. Functional authority depends on the claim or verification and acknowledgement of specialized knowledge and expert capabilities. In the case of functional authority, we have to do with practical, professional, or expert authority that depends on the acknowledgement of a superior understanding of the matter in question.

In modern societies with an extensive system of science and scholarship, it is primarily scientific and scholarly knowledge that provides the basis of functional authority. The authority of experts plays a central role in the modern circuit of what is essentially the production of knowledge in the university system, the transmission of knowledge to the various areas of social practice, and reactions and feedback from practice to science and scholarship. We may speak of professional authority with regard to the professions and vocations concerned with scientific knowledge and its transmission to the various areas of practice in society. In modern societies dependent on science, the essential significance of professional authority is recognized all the way to and including various aspects of everyday life.

Official authority has to do with the recognition of a distinct form of reflection and judgment derived from an office or position in an organization. This is a formal authority grounded in the structures and rules of organizations. Since organizations play an important part in modern societies, a central role is also acknowledged as pertaining to official authority or to authority derived from a position. The structural aspect of organizations active throughout the world also has an important function precisely in the context of a growing global society. Consequently, authority derived from office and position may also be defined as one of the main relational structures in modern global society.

Personal authority must be distinguished from functional as from official authority. Authority in the case of personal authority depends on the acknowledgement of exceptional personal qualities. It is close to the concept of charisma. Max Weber thinks of charisma as those aspects of a person which those concerned recognize as exceptional and on the basis of which such persons claim an authority which others acknowledge.[8] Weber accepts pure forms of charismatic authority as inhering only in the founding situations of communal and organizational religious formations, which are subject to a 'law' by which charisma is rendered familiar and is recast as an official charisma or an official authority. Although instances of functional and personal authority, and of authority granted by position, enter into multiple mixed forms and may support or undermine each other reciprocally, it is characteristic of the modern differentiation process to differentiate between social relationships on the basis of their dominant and evidently distinct forms of authority. Forces opposing differentiation and fusions of different forms of authority lead to specific complexes of problems in the exercise of authority.

IV. The papal office in the structure of authority in the Catholic Church

An extraordinarily high degree of centralization is an immediately evident feature of the papal office in the authority structure of the Catholic Church. The reasons for this are to be found mainly in the complexes of historical circumstances in which this centralizing organizational structure of the Catholic Church came into being.[9] The Catholic Church perceived the process of functional differentiation taking place in the nineteenth century, and the associated loss of power, as a fundamental threat to its existence, to which it reacted with a defensive concentration of all its power resources at the apex. Admittedy, the Second Vatican Council subsequently weakened the ecclesiological legitimation of centralism and also introduced an advisory collegial procedure as supplementary structural elements in the form of episcopal synods, but retained the excessive centralism.

Strange to say, a major keystone of the exercise of papal power was introduced only in the post-conciliar period. Whereas bishops and cardinals at a certain age, and while they are still alive, are forced to surrender their offices to new papal appointees, the office of the papacy is still indebted to the life-time monarchical model. Contrary, therefore, to the discussions and decisions of the Second Vatican Council on ecclesiology, the distance between the papal office and the episcopal office has been increased rather than reduced at a decisive point.

Although there is no ecclesiological doubt that the subsidiarity principle remains valid as the key element of the Church's specific social and structural teaching at least analogously, too, to its specific social form, to date there is a total lack of bases for any ecclesiological discussion of subsidiarity within the Catholic Church. Ignoring the question of which level of the Church should really call for regulation and control, papal authority is liable to, and indeed constantly does, arrogate the right to address any particular matter and to subject it to a central decision. One can imagine papal authority seriously obeying the principle of subsidiarity and seeing itself as bound to substantiate and make its own decisions only in instances when it is competent in a more appropriate because more personal sense.[10] In short, from a structural viewpoint, the danger of a constant extension and excessive appeal to papal authority is inherent in the historical growth and indeed, until now, intensification of centralism in the structure of the Catholic Church.

V. The endowment of the office with charisma and the fusion of forms of authority

From the moment of its conception in the nineteenth century, the excessively extended modern centralism of the Catholic Church has been associated with a tendency to endow the office with charisma and infuse it with authority.[11] The Pope as an individual and his extraordinary religious-charismatic characteristics and abilities are placed at the centre of the claim to authority. The formal structures of the office and the centralized decision processes are concealed by the Pope's charismatically charged image. The pontificate of Pius IX was an early high point in the loading of the papal office with charisma. One of the modes by which the continuity of the modern papacy is ensured may be seen as a degree of endowed charisma in the practice of veneration of the figure of the Pope and his sacralization as a person. In this process the particular forms of expression are considerably adapted to historical circumstances, the attitudes of the age, and technical facilities as prerequisites of its success.

New elements and an excessive emphasis on endowing the papal office
with additional charisma were observable features of the pontificate of John
Paul II. The new elements included the new role of the mass media, which
was especially evident in the media presentation of the Pope's death. No
Pope before John Paul II had made the same efforts – even to the extent of
almost breaking with tradition – to include himself as a person in the papal
office. This point has been analyzed from a sociological viewpoint on the
basis of the practice, introduced by John Paul II himself, of kissing the
ground when landing in another country.[12] The fact that John Paul II carried
out more beatifications and canonizations than in the entire previous history
of the Church may be counted as another instance of excessive recourse to
ways of making the papal office more charismatic.[13] Clearly, as events at the
time when the Pope was dying show, the extreme strategies by means of
which John Paul II made the papal office reflect his own personality and
endowed it with a charismatic aura satisified some contemporary need in a
special way.

Benedict XVI is continuing this charismatic treatment of the papal office
with his own contributions and his own profile. At all events, to date
Benedict has not carried on the ritual of kissing the ground when arriving in
another country, and has thereby distanced himself from the ritualistic,
personally imbued staging of the papal office practised by his predecessor.
The direction in which the present Pope is tending to shift the charismatic
exercise of authority is quite evident. It is the personal authority of the
scholar and intellectual that Benedict is using to shift the balance of the
scales. Contrary to his predecessor, he includes the authority of the academic and professor in the authority of the papacy, and thus gives a different
shape to the removal of distinctions from, and the fusion of authority with,
papal authority. In Benedict's case, the staging of the papacy for the media is
supplemented with references to the authority of a university professor and
a member of the worldwide 'epistemic community' of experts and scholars
that theoreticians of global society would assess as one of its constitutive
elements.[14] For Catholic theologians, obvious dangers are inherent in
Benedict's specific fusion of the forms of authority deriving from the functional authority of the scholar, the personal authority of the human individual known as Josef Ratzinger, and the official authority of the Pope. This
fusion of different types of authority is revealed on the cover of the German
edition of the first volume of the Pope's book about Jesus. Josef Ratzinger is
given as the author's name first of all, then Benedict XVI appears as the

author in much bigger letters below that. In a much-quoted passage in the Preface he refers explicitly to his personal authority in contradistinction to his official authority: 'Of course I do not need to stress the point that this book is in no sense an act of the magisterium, but only an expression of my personal quest "for the face of the Lord" (cf. Ps. 27.8). Consequently, anyone is entitled to contradict me. All I ask from my readers is that they grant me that initial sympathy that is requisite for any understanding.'[15] The Preface is followed by the dual signature of 'Josef Ratzinger – Benedict XVI'. In his book, the Pope as a scholar often represents exegetical viewpoints that are much contested among exegetes. Catholic exegetes' fears that the book and its reception could lead 'implicitly to the regulation of scholarly practice' would not seem to be unjustified.[16]

VI. Conclusion

The foregoing commentary refers to the ambivalence that is characteristic of the exercise of papal authority both in the modern era altogether and by Pope Benedict XV in particular. He has shown considerable awareness of central questions concerning religions in society as a whole throughout the world, has tackled important key topics, and has gained recognition as one of the leading actors in the international complex of religions. His exceptional intellectual abilities and his expertise as a scholar and theologian contribute to the position of authority he has achieved in the worldwide context of religions. At the same time, the way in which the papal office itself has acquired a charismatic quality and the specific fusion of forms of authority at the apex of the Church tend to reinforce the traditional inadequacy of Catholic theology in making its requisite contribution to the autonomy of the Church independently. Since theology and office are fused in a single person at the top of the Church, it is already becoming clear in the medium term that damage could be done to communication between Christian faith, the other world religions, and secular reason. The Pope's Augsburg address might well be interpreted as a first sign of this danger resulting from the papal fusion of different aspects of authority.

Translated by J.G. Cumming

Notes

1. Roland Robertson, *Globalization: Social Theory and Global Culture*, London, 1992.
2. Jürgen Habermas uses the term with reference to the persistence of religions in a secular society (*Zwischen Naturalismus und Religion*, Frankfurt am Main, 2005, pp.119–54).
3. Hartmann Tyrell, 'Singular oder Plural–Einleitende Bemerkungen zu Globalisierung und Weltgesellschaft', in Bettina Heintz, Richard Münch, & Hartmann Tyrell, *Weltgesellschaft*, special issue of *Zeitschrift für Soziologie*, Bielefeld, 2006, 1–50.
4. Cf. Karl Gabriel, '"Wenn Liebe Gestalt gewinnt". Ekklesiologische, pastorale und sozialethische Implikationen der Enzyklika', in Peter Klasvogt & Heinrich Pompey (eds), *Liebe bewegt . . . und verändert die Welt. Programmansage für eine Kirche, die liebt*, Paderborn, 2008, p. 98.
5. Josef Ratzinger, 'Was die Welt zusammenhält. Vorpolitische moralische Grundlagen eines freiheitlichen Staates', in Jürgen Habermas & Josef Ratzinger, *Dialketik der Säkularisierung. Über Vernunft und Religion*, Freiburg im Breisgau, pp. 39–60.
6. Max Weber, *Wirtschaft und Gesellschaft*, Tübingen, 1956, pp. 157–222.
7. Gerd Reinhold, *Soziologie-Lexikon*, Munich & Vienna, 1992, pp. 40–1.
8. Max Weber, *op. cit.*, pp. 179–89.
9. Karl Gabriel, Franz-Xaver Kaufmann (eds), *Zur Soziologie des Katholizismus*, Mainz, 1980, pp. 89–112, 201–25.
10. Otfried Höffe, *Vernunft und Recht*, Frankfurt am Main, 1996, pp. 220–39.
11. Ebertz, Michael, 'Herrschaft in der Kirche. Hierarchie, Tradition und Charisma im 19. Jahrhundert', in Gabriel & Kaufmann (eds), *Zur Soziologie*, *op. cit.*, pp. 108–11.
12. Hans-Georg Soeffner, *Die Ordnung der Rituale. Die Auslegung des Alltags*, 2d ed., Frankfurt am Main, n.d.
13. Agathe Bienfait, 'Zeichen und Wunder. Über die Funktion der Selig- und Heligsprechungen in der katholischen Kirche', in *Kölner Zeitschrift für Soziologie und Sozialpsychologie* 58 (2006), 1–22, esp. 2.
14. Rudolf Stichweh, 'Weltgesellschaft', in *Historisches Wörterbuch der Philosophie*, 12, Basle, 2005, cols 486–90.
15. Josef Ratzinger (Benedict XVI), *Jesus von Nazareth*, Freiburg im Breisgau, ²2007, p. 22.
16. Martin Ebner, Rudolf Hoppe & Thomas Schmeller, 'Der "historische Jesus" aus der Sicht Josef Ratzingers. Rückfragen von Neutestamentllern zum päpstlichen Jesusbuch', in: *Biblische Zeitschrift*, new series 52 (2008), pp. 648–1, esp. 64ff.

Christological Conflicts with the Magisterium

JOSÉ IGNACIO GONZÁLEZ FAUS

Given my limitations of time and space, I propose to present an overview and some criteria, rather than a detailed description of events. I begin with a parable that may seem out of place.

> An academic with a philosophical background was once attending a gathering of colleagues and there announced that he was haunted by the problem of how the universe began. Everyone referred him to the 'big bang', which by that time had progressed from a hypothesis to a scientific certainty. Our academic persisted, saying that what really worried him was what caused the big bang. The official replies repeated that the big bang had no cause, or that it was its own cause. Not satisfied with these replies, the academic widened the field of his search, came across the Bible (virtually unknown in Western circles at that time), and worked out an answer in which he spoke of God as Creator, perhaps with some deficiencies in his manner of explaining the Bible, on which he was no expert.
>
> The scientific community reacted harshly: he was called an enemy of science and accused of being a 'creationist' (a pejorative term in those days owing to various stupid abuses made of it) and was told that Laplace had already answered Napoleon saying that he had 'no need of the God hypothesis to build his theories'. The academic tried to explain that he was asking on a *different and higher plane* than Napoleon. But his colleagues brushed this response aside, and our academic was finally roundly condemned by the scientific community.

The parable is designed to show that the temptation to provide answers without listening to the question is not the exclusive preserve of faith, or of the Church, but is inherent in human thought. Underlying this, I should still like to evoke what Ratzinger says in the prologue to his book on Jesus, when he asks his readers for 'that initial goodwill without which no understanding is possible'. Words similar to those of Ignatius of Loyola at the start of his *Spiritual Exercises*, advising that 'every Christian must be more disposed to agree with his neighbour's proposal than to condemn it; and if he cannot agree with it, let him ask him how he understands it'. What Ignatius sets out as a Christian obligation, Ratzinger proposes as a human prerequisite. But the content is practically the same.

This double presupposition should be useful for what this article seeks to provide: an overview of the conflicts between Rome and current christologies. Given the impossibility of producing a catalogue – which I am in any case not equipped to do – it seems to me that these can be reduced to three headings: Rome fears that the divinity of Christ is being denied in current christologies, or at least being reduced to 'Arian' levels. It fears historical research about Jesus. And it fears that the uniqueness of Jesus is being compromised through discussion of the relationship between Christianity and the world religions. The first conflict can be exemplified in the Notification against Jon Sobrino; the second in the attacks, in Spain, on the splendid book by J. A. Pagola,[1] while the third concerns very well known names: Dupuis and Haight to name but two.

I. The divinity of Jesus

The first conflict is exemplified in the parable recounted above. This is confirmed by an anecdote told me by its protagonist. Over twenty-five years ago, a religious who had problems with the Roman Curia over a book on Jesus Christ was summoned to Rome by the general of his Order, who arranged an interview for him with a member of the CDF. The interview was cordial, and during it the Monsignor said, 'But, father, why do people like you persist in writing books of christology? Everything in christology's been said! Confine yourselves to repeating the teaching of the councils, and all's well. But, of course, if you insist on saying new things, you will inevitably fall into error. . . .'

In my view, the good monsignor had failed to understand that, however valid the conciliar formulas may be, a multiplicity of new approaches and questions have arisen today. The most basic pastoral contact shows us that the conciliar formulas – to limit ourselves to them – now do more harm than good: the most they can do is *impart information*, but they fail to summon anyone to a *change of life*. And a faith that does not invite a change of life may be a belief but is not 'faith' in the justifying sense of the word. When

Bonhoeffer wrote that the workman who said, 'Jesus was a good man', was perhaps saying more than him when he upheld one person and two natures, he was indicating just this. Because, for the workman, saying that Jesus was 'good' was a call to change, while repeating that in Jesus there were one subsistence and two natures contributed nothing to his life. Luther had seen as much earlier: in the time of Arius, 'the article of the Trinity could be spirit', but 'the spirit and the letter change with the times: what was nourishment to others is a dead letter to us'.[2]

This is what, as I see it, Rome fails to perceive, and what gives rise to useless conflicts. The way they are approached is useless, and so is the means sought to resolve them: the theological community is today broad enough for any debatable or imprecise statement to provoke confrontation and debate in the bosom of the church community immediately. And such discussion is, human nature being what it is, the only way of progressing toward truth. Truth cannot be imposed by those who believe they already possess it.

This failure to understand the problem often places the Roman authorities in a position of antecedent mistrust, which is another way of not understanding the answer.[3] In this respect it has to be said that the CDF is today leaning dangerously in the direction of a sort of Monophysitism that, as Rahner observed some time ago, is the easiest direction in which to falsify faith in the divinity of Jesus Christ and is 'latent in the minds of many Christians' (and of many monsignors). In Jesus, divinity and humanity make up a balance that becomes enormously unstable when we try to enclose it in words. It is notable that Rome has not been on the alert to condemn the frequent implicit denials of Jesus' true humanity ('like us in all things but sin') that are presently swarming through the church community. This imbalance rings alarm bells for me. And it leads me to the second point I want to make.

II. Historical criticism

As mentioned above, there has been a veritable crusade mounted very quickly in Spain against J. A. Pagola's splendid book on Jesus. Even a bishop has made an unfortunate intervention in the polemic (which may be more self-seeking than objective). The accusation is always the same: 'This book does not accord with the faith of the Church'.

But what Pagola wrote was a book about *his faith* in Jesus. As the title shows, it merely deals with 'an historical approach' (and a very valuable one it is). There is room for debate with him on the level of historical approaches (I would dissent in some cases), but not on the level of faith, which Pagola continues to profess in calm and serenity.[4]

Why then do some people see it as contrary to the faith of the Church? On account of a procedure that I denounced as unacceptable many years ago: *you start from a preconceived idea of God, and you argue that because God is like that, Jesus has to be such and such.* . . . Unconsciously, the procedure robs Jesus of his character as revealer (Word) of God, and renders impossible what Bonhoeffer noted with a believer's subtlety: 'The God who is revealed in Jesus overturns the ideas religious people have of God'. This is inconvenient and requires a lot of conversion. As a friend said to me about this case: 'What has happened is that Pagola has discovered a Jesus without power. And for all those who can only conceive of God as power, it seems impossible for this Jesus to be God'.

This is a popular expression of the matter. In more technical terms, I fear that many official statements by my Church give expression to an innate denial of the self-emptying (*kenosis*) of God in Jesus. Unwittingly, they show no interest in a God who empties himself of his divine image in his relationship with human beings and who acts not in accordance with his divine rights but denying himself these rights, 'although he was a Son' (cf. Heb. 5:8). And this is problematic, since it would oblige the ecclesiastical authorities to make the transcendent dimension not a weapon capable of making things easier for them but an awkward imperative forcing them to identify more closely with the difficulties of the human condition.

Finally, there is another element in the criticisms of Pagola's Jesus that strikes me as dangerous. Ratzinger speaks of the convergence between reason and faith, and I agree with his words addressed to the university of Rome: 'keeping sensitivity to the truth alive.'[5] But if one denies viability to what scientific investigation into Jesus is producing (duly compared and within its limited possibilities), this compatibility between faith and reason undergoes major breakdowns. This why we need to ask, quoting Ratzinger once again, if what lies behind these accusations is truly the scandal of faith, which cannot be eliminated, or the scandal of our own laziness taking refuge in it so as to avoid problems. John Dominic Crossan, in a polemical – and certainly debatable on some historical points – book, rightly states: 'I cannot see that there is any contradiction whatsoever between the historical Jesus and defining him as Christ, meaning: no idea of the original was betrayed by converting the Jesus of history into Christ. Another quite separate question is whether any idea was betrayed by putting Jesus into the hands of Constantine.'⁶

Curiously, the Roman Curia, in many of its interventions, seems to disregard what the magisterium has taught about modern methods of biblical research.⁷

III. The uniqueness of Jesus Christ and world religions

My final point is one that demonstrates a more urgent need to understand that we are facing new problems and that the road to the promised land leads through the desert and not back to Egypt. Those who confess that 'there is no other name under heaven . . . by which we must be saved' (Acts 4.12) and at the same time profess that God 'desires everyone to be saved' (1 Tim. 2.4) are faced with the obligation to seek a theology of world religions. I say 'religions' because salvation does not come about exclusively through the individual route of one's own conscience but also through the community routes provided by our social setting. The Muslim I once heard tell me that for him I was no more than an 'infidel' and that his religion ordered him to eliminate all infidels will be faced with other problems that Muslims have to resolve among themselves (because I know that they do not all think like that).

Once again, it is vital for Rome to understand that this problem is new and is still not resolved. And that we cannot say more than preliminary words about it, and that the help God gives the Church does not provide it with a convenient dispensation from the task of seeking the truth. Furthermore, this help may not come directly through a mitre; it may come through those simple souls who, to Jesus' joy, understand the things of God better than the wise (cf. Matt. 11.27). At a time of provisional first words on the subject, errors are bound to be made. Personally, I feel disquiet at the solution suggested by some, that we should abandon the divinity of Jesus understood as incarnation of the Word of God, so that Christianity can present itself on a level playing field with other religions. On a different tack, the Indian Jesuit Michael Amaladoss attributes many Eastern titles to Jesus (including avatar of God) while staying strictly within the limits of orthodoxy.⁸ In my latest book I tried to show – how successfully I do not know – that there is a way of confessing Jesus' divinity fully without placing Christianity on a higher level but rather on a lower one in the forum of religions. And that the religions will only be able to come together in a 'theologal anthropocentrism' that is at once enormously Christian and universally human.⁹

I have to declare that I cannot consider the quick and easy methods of the CDF – abolishing professorships, prohibiting publications, and so on – Christian. Such authoritarianism has so little of theology about it that it can hardly be christological. Among us, truth never has virgin births but sees the light in a sea of mess that can only be cleaned away once the child is born. Dialogue between theologians and representatives of the magisterium is the only way to bring this difficult and painful birth about, and the best aid to theologians who have gone astray. The 'Holy Office' should have learned from the case of Teilhard de Chardin. There were points that needed to be qualified and re-situated among his brilliant intuitions, and this could have been done if his books had been published in his lifetime, so coming into the hands of the scientific and theological community.

In the particular case of christology, any believer, and especially church authorities, are obliged to act 'christologically' if their actions are to have any credibility. This means 'not break[ing] a bruised reed or quench[ing] a smouldering wick' (Matt. 12.20). In my humble opinion, this is what the church authorities do with excessive frequency. The argument that worldly ways of exercising authority are the only effective ones for something as important as safeguarding the faith strikes me as an argument from 'little faith', prohibited by Jesus when he ordered that 'among you it should not be like that'.

Translated by Paul Burns

Notes

1. *Jesús de Nazaret. Una aproximación histórica*, Madrid: PPC, 2007. The book sold 30,000 copies in its first four months.
2. WA, 4, 365. On the possibility of 'repatriating' the full value possibly contained in the conciliar formulas concerning Jesus, I refer to the chapter on 'dogmatic christology and struggle for justice' in my *Fe en Dios y construcción de la historia* (Madrid, 1998).
3. If I may be allowed a private anecdote: when we were preparing the 'Commentary on the Notification by the CDF on the christology of Jon Sobrino' at the 'Christianity and Justice' study centre in Barcelona, one of the participants commented: 'As a professor of theology, I have to say that if a pupil had presented such a text in an exam, I think I should have had to fail him'.
4. At the public launch of his book in Barcelona, Pagola declared that he had tried not to take account of his faith in writing the book – but that the book had not damaged his faith in any way.

5. *El País*, 17 Jan. 2008.
6. *The Historical Jesus: the Life of a Mediterranean Jewish Peasant*, Edinburgh: T & T. Clark, 1993 (here quoting from Sp. trans., p. 485).
7. As shown in the 'Christianity and Justice' Commentary on the Notification concerning Jon Sobrino.
8. *The Asian Jesus*, Maryknoll, NY: Orbis Books, 2006.
9. See *El rostro humano de Dios. De la revolución de Jesús a la divinidad de Jesús*, Santander: Sal Terrae, 2007.
10. In *La autoridad de la verdad. Momentos oscuros del magisterio eclesiástico* (Santander: Sal Terrae, ²2007), I have tried to show what these christological criteria for action would be (in Part 2) and how not holding to them has often led ecclesiastical authority in the long run into somewhat unfortunate situations that contribute to its current discredit.

The Pope's Book on Jesus: Conflicting Interpretations

ROSINO GIBELLINI

Written over the course of three years, the first volume of the Pope's awaited book *Jesus of Nazareth*, which reconstructs Jesus' ministry from his baptism in the Jordan to the transfiguration, is dated 30 September 2006 (the Feast of St Jerome).[1] There is a second volume in preparation, which is proving 'more difficult from a historical point of view' (Stuhlmacher).[2] The book bears a double signature, Joseph Ratzinger and Pope Benedict XVI, but involves only the first – the theologian, that is, and not the pope: 'I do not think it is necessary to say expressly that this book is not at all a magisterial act but the expression of my personal seeking of the "Lord's face" (see Ps. 27.8). Therefore everyone has the liberty to contradict me' (p. 20). A singular event and a singular admission. This is the first time that a pope has written a book on Jesus, let alone made a clear distinction between his writing and his authority. The singular admission could, as has generally been predicted and noted, have positive consequences for the ever-problematic relationship between the exercise of the magisterium and theological research. The event could even usher in a new phase of constructive dialogue between these two ecclesial entities at the service of the church community and of society.

The Pope asks only for 'that initial sympathy (*Sympathie*) without which there is no possible understanding' (p. 20). Schleiermacher himself, the founder of modern hermeneutics, incidentally asked rather for an identification (*Einfühlung*) of the interpreter with the author's thought as a condition for understanding. The sympathy asked by the Pope has been abundantly granted by exegetes and theologians, who have read and re-read and only then written, expressing agreements, putting forward clarifications and criticisms, formulating a degree of dissent.

The Pope's *Jesus of Nazareth* is required reading. This advice is given by the evangelical theologian Eberhard Jüngel to his Christian flock but also to his 'atheistically socialized' nieces and nephews in the former GDR, to his young friends – Christian, half-Christian, atheist. He repeats Augustine's words in his *Confessions*: *tolle, legi*, even though the learned theologian from Tübingen knows that Augustine's Latin words referred to the scriptures and not to a work by a Catholic, let alone one written by a pope. Jüngel recognizes that in making this recommendation to his young friends, he is 'paying the greatest complement possible to a work of theology.' It is a book that will make them more thoughtful; furthermore, they will receive 'a vivid impression' of the person who is the central point of reference for all the Christian communities. Ratzinger asks himself what Jesus brought. And, as Jüngel reads it, he answers, in what is the book's central thesis, that Jesus 'brought God'; but in this way, quoting Tillich, he touches on the 'supreme and unconditional concern' that inspires every human being. And young readers too are bound to be interested by it. But is there not something suspicious about this advice (Jüngel cunningly insinuates), coming as it does from a professor at the university of Tübingen, recommending a book written by a former professor at the same university, who at his meeting with the great Russian writer Soloviev granted a doctorate *honoris causa* in theology to none other than the 'Antichrist'? However suspicious it might be, the recommendation to read is authoritatively given and authoritatively justified.[3]

What sort of book has the theologian-pope written? How might it be defined? Among definitions offered, we might choose that by the long-time, internationally renowned exegete Franz Mussner, professor emeritus of theology and New Testament exegesis at the university of Regensburg: 'a book about relationships'. He indicates five: 1. the basic relationship shown in the book is that of the Son to the Father; 2. then, it establishes relationships between the theme of the book and similar relationships to be found in the Gospels and the New Testament; 3. it emphasizes the close relationship between Old and New Testaments; 4. the treatment follows in relationship to the Fathers of the Church; 5. it also, however, relates to the day-to-day situation of the world, as shown in the treatment of the Beatitudes, which are brought up to date.[4]

Even though Eberhard Jüngel advises his young friends to skip the Introduction at a first reading (but to come back to it on a second), biblicists and theologians are reading it with close attention, since it is there that the methods followed in this re-reading of the figure of Jesus are formulated.

Any research into Jesus, which involves the Bible, cannot depart from the historical method: 'Let me state at the outset that the historical method –

owing simply to the intrinsic nature of theology and faith – is and remains an essential dimension of exegetical work. Because for biblical faith, in fact, reference to real historical events is fundamental' (p. 11). But then the limits of the historical method are immediately indicated 'because it finds itself challenged by the Bible' (p. 12): *first*, in that it considers the past and leaves the past to speak; *second*, its object is human speech strictly as human, even if it can perhaps intuit the 'added value' enclosed in the speech of the past; *third*, it cannot grasp, or at least not immediately, the unity of all those books known collectively as 'Bible'. The historical method, then, needs to be integrated with others. What is needed above all is to view the Bible in its entirety, as the sum total of all the books of which it is composed, by practising a 'canonical exegesis' (p. 14), though not the sort of canonical exegesis that regards the sum total of all the books of the Bible as literature, but rather a canonical exegesis that becomes 'theological exegesis' (p. 15), that regards the Bible as Holy Scripture, and is able to see Jesus Christ as the key to it all: 'Certainly, christological hermeneutics, which sees the key to everything in Jesus Christ and, starting from him, learns to understand the Bible as a unity, presupposes a decision in faith and cannot derive from the historical method alone' (p. 15).

The Pope, therefore, accepts the *historical method* as a necessary basis, but integrates it and moves beyond it in a *canonical exegesis*, practised as a *theological exegesis*, which brings about a *christological hermeneutics*. We are, then, looking at a complex method made up, as we have seen, of four conceptions, or four steps to take, the last two of which involve the intervention of faith.

Historians of Christian origins know that the two decades from 30 AD, the probable date of the crucifixion, and 50 AD, the approximate date of the Council of Jerusalem and the appearance of the first writings that were to form the New Testament, are the most obscure years they have to study. They saw the formation of christology, which interpreted Jesus solely starting from the mystery of God. But, according to theology, it was formed on the basis of what had gone before. And so, Ratzinger writes: 'Is it not more logical, also from the historical point of view, that greatness be found in the origin and that the figure of Jesus break all available categories and thus be understood only from the mystery of God?' (pp. 18–19). Continuing this – historical-theological – course, Ratzinger then clarifies: 'I have sought to make the attempt to present the Jesus of the Gospels as the real Jesus, as the "historical Jesus" in the real, true sense' (p. 18).

The Pope's book presupposes the historico-critical method but moves beyond it: it is the work of a 'systematic theologian, who practises biblical exegesis', whose main, if not exclusive concern is to pursue research into the 'theology of Jesus'; it is therefore a 'narrative dogmatics' or a 'narrative christology'.[5] Rudolph Pesch also sees the basis for the construction of the book as 'undoubtedly a dogmatic-systematic basis'.[6] A clear indication of this is his use of the Gospel of John. The historical method concentrates rather on the Synoptic Gospels, referring to the Gospel of John for any needed relevant material. Ratzinger, on the other hand, uses John's Gospel at length, which he attributes, even with his extensive knowledge of the 'Johannine question', to an eye-witness. This is a key point not shared by many biblical scholars and theologians. Eberhard Jüngel writes: 'That the Prologue to John's Gospel is the product of a "post-paschal" reflection in faith, even Ratzinger could not deny. But his process of argumentation runs the risk of failing to see the individual trees for the dense wood. Postulating the "inner unity of scripture" is in no way illegitimate, but it has to be far more complex, richer in tensions, and laden with problems than Ratzinger's book would lead one to suspect.'[7] It may, though, surprise many people, from a Catholic and ecumenical point of view, that a book written by a dogmatic theologian should be so interwoven with the Bible and exegesis. To which one can apply the words of the Erfurt Catholic exegete Heinz Schürmann: 'To the question: Is he an exegete or a theologian? I should like to ripost: Is he a pianist or a musician?'[8]

The inspiration for the Pope's book is *The Lord* by Romano Guardini (1949), in that this set out an image of Jesus 'as he lived on earth and as, while being wholly man, he at the same time brought God to us' (p. 7). But he is not indulging in nostalgia: while the Italian-German writer may have been unaware of the historico-critical method, Ratzinger has in turn 're-worked it and sought to move beyond it. This lends interest to his work for New Testament scholars of today.'[9]

But it would also be appropriate to cite von Balthasar: according to Knut Backhaus, a Catholic exegete from Munich, the Pope's book provides an 'aesthetic-of-Christ', in that it puts von Balthasar's method of 'perceiving the figure' (*Gestalt*) of Christ into practice. It is therefore a different work from one of historical research, even if it has a historical-narrative structure. Backhaus astutely observes: 'With this book, historical research into Jesus has not produced any new outcomes, but neither has it been brought to any conclusion.'[10] In other words: the Pope's book has not made any contribution to historico-critical methods, but it has not put a stop to further contributions to this method from other sources and following other methodologies.

One might say that Ratzinger's Jesus is set against Harnack's liberal Jesus: on this point Ratzinger has already expressed himself in the book-interview *God and the World* (2000),[11] but Jan-Heiner Tück, a dogmatic theologian from Osnabrück, has expressed this still more directly and incisively, stating that in Ratzinger's reconstruction, 'Even the Son belongs to the gospel'.[12]

I mentioned earlier the four steps required by Ratzinger's methodology. Jörg Frei, an Evangelical biblicist from Munich, reduces them to three: the Pope proceeds 'historically, canonically, ecclesially'. He concludes his close analysis by saying: 'The basic christological task, which Ratzinger pursues in this work (disregarding many corrections that can be made of details), is theologically urgent and exegetically perfectly well founded', but it should be said that exegetes, as exegetes, proceed in an another manner, differing from the dogmatic method, because they are more attentive to distinctions among the texts, besides their possible correspondences, but also to justified theological differences.[13]

It is, however, worth noting that Ratzinger takes a severely critical line toward the historico-critical method, and this is still incomprehensible for many professionals, both Catholic and Protestant. The Catholic biblicist Rudolf Hoppe, of Bonn University, writes: 'His verdict on a consistent historico-critical approach is frankly incomprehensible, even if he then pronounces it "indispensable" [. . .]. Is Joseph Ratzinger the theologian not here undervaluing the great potential represented by historical research and presentation of traditions of Jesus, beyond all insuperable limits? [. . .] In any case a new "turn" (*Runde*) is now coming about in historical research into Jesus'.[14]

How to account for this diffidence in approaching the historical method? Martin Ebner, a Catholic exegete from Münster, speaks of 'fear of the multiplicity of images of Jesus' to which the historical approach might lead; of 'fear of coming into contact with the social aspect', which would explain the book's concentration on the discourses instead of on the miracle stories and the table community with publicans and sinners; and 'fear of facing up to the actual origins', and hence to the lines of development that, sometimes in contradictory fashion, have led to what is now the true religion-community'.[15]

Thomas Söding, a member of the International Theological Commission, an exegete from Wuppertal, who deserves credit for having brought German

New Testament scholars together to discuss the theologian-pope's book, recalls the 'agreeable ingenuousness' that makes Ratzinger declare *in limine libri*: 'I trust in the gospel' (p. 17), but the exegetes' comment was that, 'Critical research into just how far this trust can be justified is and always will be the task of New Testament exegetes and their historical researches into Jesus'. Rounding off the contributions, Söding writes: 'The heart of the discussion, which always surfaced in the various replies, touched on the relationship between theology and historical criticism, between event and memory, between revelation and narrative.'[16]

These problems keep recurring, as Karl Rahner often remarked. While Blondel wrote *History and Dogma* in 1904, at the very height of the Modernist crisis, the problem has now become more complex and appears as 'history, revelation, dogma', but Christian theology now has the instruments to approach it in a different way, starting from both exegesis and dogmatics: from an exegesis that has the necessary contact s with dogmatics, and from a dogmatics that grants exegetical research the same 'sympathy' it asks for its own systematic reflection.[17]

Translated by Paul Burns

Notes

1. See J. Ratzinger/Benedict XVI, *Jesus von Nazareth – Von der Taufe im Jordan bis zu Verklärung*, Freiburg, Basle, Vienna: Herder, 2007; Eng. trans. *Jesus of Nazareth: from the Baptism in the Jordan to the Transfiguration*, New York: Doubleday; London: Bloomsbury, 2007. (Page refs. here are to the Italian edition, Milan: Rizzoli, 2007.
2. P. Stuhlmacher, 'Joseph Ratzingers Jesus-Buch – ein bedeutsamer geistlicher Wegweiser' in J.-H. Tück (ed.), *Annäherungen an 'Jesus von Nazareth'. Das Buch des Papstes in der Diskussion*, Ostfildern: Grünewald, 2007, p. 30.
3. Cf. E. Jüngel, 'Der hypothetische Jesus. Anmerkungen zum Jesus-Buch des Papstes', in Tück, *op. cit.*, pp. 94–103.
4. Cf. F. Mussner, 'Ein Buch der Beziehung', in Th. Söding (ed.), *Das Jesus-Buch des Papstes. Die Antwort der Neutestamentler*, Freiburg: Herder, 2007, pp. 87–98.
5. Th. Söding, 'Auf der Suche nach dem Anlitz des Herren', in *idem, op. cit.*, pp. 134–56.
6. R. Pesch, '"Der Jesus der Evangelien ist auch der einzing wirkliche historische Jesus". Anmerkungen zum Konstructionspinckt des Jesus-Buch', in Tüch, *op. cit.*, p. 40.
7. Jüngel, *op. c it.*, p. 101.

8. Quoted by R. Kampling, 'Jede Kontroverse um des Himmels Willen trägt bleibende Früchte (Pirke Avot 5.19)', in Söding, *op. cit.*, p. 75.
9. Söding, p. 136, n. 5.
10. K. Backhaus, 'Christus-Ästethetik', in Söding, pp. 20–9.
11. Cf. J. Ratzinger, *Gott und die Welt. Glauben und Leben in in serer Zeit. Ein Gespräch mit Peter Seewald*, Munich, Knaur, n.e. 2005, p. 218. Eng. trans, *God and the World. A Conversation with Peter Seewald*, San Francisco: Ignatius Press, 2000
12. J. H. Tück, 'Auch der Sohn gehört in das Evangelium', in *idem, op. cit.*, pp. 155–81.
13. Cf. J. Frei, 'Hisotrisch-kanonisch-kirchlich: Zum Jesusbild Joseph Ratzingers', in Söding, pp. 43–53.
14. R. Hoppe, 'Historische Rückfrage und deutende Reinnerung an Jesus', in Söding, pp. 62–3.
15. Cf. M. Ebner, 'Jeder Ausleger hat seine blinden Flecken', in Söding, pp. 30–42.
16. Söding, p. 145.
17. On Ratzinger's theology in general see H. Verweyen, *Joseph Ratzinger – Benedikt XVI. Die Entwicklung seines Denkens*, Darmstatt: WGB, 2007. On the relationship between his theology and his book on Jesus see *idem*, 'Kanonische Exegese und historische Kritik. Zum inhaltlichen und methodischen Ort des Jesus-Buches', in J.-H. Tück, *op. cit.*, pp. 155–81.

For a first attempt at a bibliography on the reception of the Pope's book see G. Anger & J.-H. Tück, 'Vorstudien und Echo. Ein erster bibliographischer Überblick zu Joseph Ratzingers *Jesus von Nazareth*', in Tück, *op. cit.*, pp. 182–99. Among the vast bibliography note the volume (with some very critical contributions), '*Jesus von Nazareth' controvers. Rückfragen an Joseph Ratzinger* (Theologie actuell, vol. II), Münster: Lit, 2007. Hans Küng's contribution in particular claims that as a theologian Ratzinger always appeals to tradition: his interpretative key to the Bible is the Hellenistic councils of the fifth century; starting from these, he interprets John's Gospel, and on the basis of John he then interprets the Synoptics. The result is a top-down christology, as opposed to the bottom-up christology practised by Küng. But this leads straight into the overall christological debate.

The Forthcoming Synod on the Word of God

SILVIA SCATENA

By the time this issue of *Concilium* appears, the *Instrumentum laboris* prepared for discussion at the Twelfth Ordinary General Assembly of the Synod of Bishops, scheduled for October 2008, drawn up on the basis of replies to the Questionnaire in the Consultitative Document – the *Lineamenta* – sent in April 2007 to bishops' conferences, to the synods of the Eastern Catholic Churches *sui juris*, to the dicasteries of the Roman Curia, and to the Union of Superiors General, will already have been distributed.[1] Devoted to 'The Word of God in the life and mission of the Church', the forthcoming synod will resume discussion of a subject that is obviously crucial to the *aggiornameto* sought by the council, the object of impassioned debates and pronouncements prolonged up to the morrow of the promulgation of *Dei verbum*.[2] Almost fifty years on from Vatican II, the main object of the synodal discussions will be to make an assessment of the process of reception of the dogmatic constitution on the Word of God, a process on which the *Lineamenta* requested an overall evaluation, from a 'predominantly pastoral' standpoint', bearing in mind 'the many positive results brought about among the People of God' but no less the 'still open and problematic' aspects. The principal objective set out for the Synod will in effect be to 'promote a correct hermeneutical use of Scripture, to provide good guidance for the necessary process of evangelization and inculturation', to 'encourage ecumenical dialogue, strictly linked to hearing the Word of God', and 'to favour Jewish-Christian encounter and dialogue, and more broadly, inter-religious and inter-cultural dialogue'.

The prospect of a wide-ranging discussion on a central point in the process of reception of the council has nevertheless been damaged by restrictive doctrinal and procedural interventions that have prevented the Churches as a whole from playing an effective part in the synodal process.[3] The limited capacity of episcopal conferences to intervene in the preparatory phase, through not sharing in the preparation of the *Lineamenta*; their ability to intervene only individually and privately in the devising of the *Instrumentum laboris*; their lack of involvement in the choice of members of various bodies; then the general closure to the outside world and difficulty of communicating with the media – all militate against a participatory climate surrounding the preparation of the synod. Even though the October assembly's subject matter has been suggested over several years by various bishops and institutions, this time too the publication of the *Lineamenta* has met with little attention, and, with the exception of a few official initiatives, involving limited numbers of 'experts on the subject',[4] the start of the synodal process has gone relatively unnoticed. In this context, however, some waves have been made by the 'prognosis' for the forthcoming synod suggested by Cardinal Martini, published last February in *La Civiltà Cattolica*:[5] a prognosis that includes fears that the delicate balance of various elements that can be traced in the *Lineamenta* might presage a re-reading of *Dei Verbum* not commensurate with its language, using formulae that 'would represent a step backwards with respect to the Second Vatican Council', which 'with great care and in well-chosen phrases' has already 'amply' expressed 'what the Church feels about divine revelation and about the Word of God, including that contained in scripture, as well as about tradition.'

The succession, over the course of a few months, of Benedict XVI's *motu proprio* on greater freedom to use the pre-conciliar rite, then the five questions and answers from the CDF on teaching on the Church and interpretation of *Lumen gentium* 8, then the *Note on Some Aspects of Evangelization*, which touches on some delicate points in *Dignitatis humanae*, would seem to suggest, in effect, an intention comprehensively to review significant advances made by the conciliar magisterium. In this case, such a re-reading could affect what the council had agreed on such basic issues as the relationship between scripture and tradition or the question of how scripture was to be interpreted, a point on which the Pontifical Biblical Commission had amply dwelt in its 1993 instruction on 'Interpretation of the Bible in the Church'.[6] The words of the rapporteur-general of the synod, Archbishop Ouellet of Quebec – who in an interview given last January had noted that 'a question on which the synod should seek to provide a word of clarification concerns the interpretation of the Sacred Scriptures' – point clearly in such a direction.[7]

It is above all the status of historico-critical exegesis that appears to be the main object of reappraisal: while on one hand the historico-critical method itself is no longer the object of debate, on the other reference to the fruits of biblical studies and of exegesis is always accompanied in the *Lineamenta* by repeated indications of the risks of arbitrary, reductive, ideological, or 'simply human' interpretations, of their inadequacy and therefore of the need to move beyond them, 'correctly unifying the historico-literal meaning and the theological-spiritual meaning.'[8] This tendency includes frequent reminders of the competence of the magisterium in interpretation of the Word of God, insistence on the 'specific role' of the *Catechism of the Catholic Church* as a 'sure guide for the teaching of the faith', and recommendations to integrate the historico-critical method 'with other forms of approach' – in particular with that 'canonical exegesis' founded on unitary consideration of the biblical text received as the rule of faith for a believing community that would favour – in the words of Benedict XVI to the Swiss bishops in November 2006 – 'a spiritual reading, which is not a separate edifying exercise, but rather an internal immersion in the presence of the Word'. There is a strong insistence here on the spiritual dimension of scripture, not to mention an assertion of the necessary connection between an exegetical undertaking and a hermeneutical one 'according to the mind of the Church' and with close consideration given to the guidelines laid down by the magisterium. In the first place, there an absence or at least a blurring of any emphasis on the anti-fundamentalist function of historico-critical exegesis, on the importance of the part it should play in liturgy, in pastoral work, and in community activities, or on the contribution contextual exegesis can make especially to matters of debate. Besides this, there is virtually no hint of any introduction of renewal or of the 'continual conversion' of the Church required by the Spirit through the Word, which might have given some backing to the synod's declared objective of encouraging ecumenical dialogue.

In general, then, the impression given is one of diminishing the import of the passage of *Dei verbum* 10 on the magisterium being 'not superior to the word of God but [. . .] rather its servant', and of a re-positioning of the value and ecclesial function of exegetical research – a re-positioning made more explicit in the presentation of the *Lineamenta* by the under-secretary of the synod, Mgr Frezza, who has emphasized the need to reconsider 'the reality of the Church's teaching body' as the 'authentic heir to the apostolic teaching body at the beginnings' and to reject 'the irritant of new teachings and part-time teachers'; also by the secretary, Mgr Eterović, who has stressed the importance of approaching scripture through the four traditional means, 'welcoming the positive results of the historico-critical method but at the same time overcoming its limitations'.[9] A tendency, this, that they both effectively recognize in Ratzinger/Benedict XVI's *Jesus of Nazareth*, which the secretary-general of the CEI, Mgr Bertoni, has also singled out as being 'the best answer to how historical research can stand alongside faith and, with regard to Jesus, prove capable of providing him with a far more note-worthy face than the mutilated and insignificant one, concealed among the average ones of his time, that certain persons of culture and historians of Christianity, badly guided by their ideological involvements, can put forward.'[10]

Presented as 'an active and effective gesture concerning the "reception of the Council, in which everything depends on right interpretation or on its correct hermeneutics"',[11] the *Lineamenta* seem built on a foundation of out-right undervaluation of, if not contempt for, the products and the purposes of exegetical research. Such an undervaluation can hardly help in resolving the problem of the poverty of biblical understanding and the inadequate familiarity with scripture shown by the majority of the faithful, let alone in nourishing a dynamism in resolving the tensions in research into the gospel truth.[12]

Translated by Paul Burns

Notes

1. The text of the *Lineamenta* is available in various languages at www.vatican.va.
2. On the complex history of the composition of *Dei verbum* see R. Burigana, *La Bibbia nel concilio*, Bologna, 1998. On the fate of some variants introduced into chance announcements and concerning expressions to which some doctrinal points debated at length were subtended, allow me to refer to my 'La filologia delle decisioni conciliari: dal voto in congregazione generale alla *Editio typica*', in J. Doré and A. Melloni (eds), *Volti di fine concilio. Studi di storia e telogia sulla conclusione del Vaticano II*, Bologna, 1999, pp. 53–97.
3. On this point I recommend the work by A. Indelicato, *Il Sinodo dei vescovi: la collegialità sospesa*, shortly to be published by the Il Mulino Press.
4. I refer, for example, to the 'study Convention in preparation for the synod' held at the beginning of last December under the auspices of the Pontifical University of the Lateran and to the congress held in Barcelona, also in December 2007, at the Faculty of Theology of Catalonia, on the subject of 'Word of God, Word on God'. One can also point to the correlation between the theme of the synod and the subject of the Lenten meditations preached by Fr Cantalamessa for the pope and the curia: 'The word of God is living and active (Heb. 4.12)'.

5. Cf. C. M. Martini, 'Il prossimo Sinodo dei vescovi sulla Parola di Dio'. *La Civiltà Cattolica* I (2008), 217–23.

6. For the text of which see *Enchiridion Vaticanum*, 13, *Documenti ufficiali della Santa Sede 1991–1993*, Bologna, 1995, p. 1554–733.

7. 'An interpretation that cannot be purely individual', Ouellet continued, 'but must always be conformed to the living tradition of the Church. An interpretation, then, that, while giving the scientific research of exegetes its due, must not place itself in competition with or opposition to the magisterium.' Cf. G. Cardinale, 'Ouellet: nel Sinodo dialogo e misione', *Avvenire*, 31 Jan. 2008.

8. On the same lines see also L. Prezzi, 'La Chiesa e la *Dei Verbum*', *Il Regno* 10 (2007), 290.

9. The addresses by Mgr Eterović and Mgr Frezza on 27 Apr. 2007 can also be found at www.vatican.va.

10. Cf. G. Betori, *Leggere la Bibbia nella Chiesa. Dalla* Dei Verbum *a oggi*, Cinisello Balsamo, 2000, pp. 59–60.

11. Cf. the address by Mgr Frezza, citing Benedict's XVI's discourse to the Roman Curia on 22 Dec. 2005.

12. On this see also A. Melloni's marginal comments to Cardinal Martini's analysis of Ratzinger's book on Jesus, 'La fatica degli interprete non si può liquidare d'ufficio', *Corriere della Sera*, 25 May 2007.

Images of Jesus in Contemporary Cultures

ROBERT SCHREITER

One of the most interesting developments at the point of intersection between new developments in christology and the inculturation movement of the last thirty years has been the profusion of new images of Jesus. Images are central to the Christian imagination and sensibility: they convey an array of ideas, feelings, and memories that may elude more abstract conceptualization of who Jesus Christ is for us. Images often shape our identities much more strongly than do concepts.

In many oral cultures, 'face' carries the connotations that are associated with the concept 'identity'. The importance of understanding 'faces of Jesus' is a special avenue of insight into the quality of people's lives of faith. Even in mainly literate cultures, there has been a renewed interest in some sectors in the face of Jesus, as can be seen in the devotion to the 'divine face' of Jesus being promoted by the Vatican.

The face or image of Jesus provides a perspective into the humanity of Jesus. As we shall see shortly, many of the images of Jesus that have emerged in recent years try to draw Jesus into the matrix of the cultures of those who promote such an image. But that human image is also a window into divinity. A corollary of the Christian confession of the full divinity and humanity of Jesus is that we receive our best insight into what is divinity and what is humanity by looking to Jesus. Contemporary images of Jesus refract for us precisely those possibilities.

This article will explore some of the contemporary images of Jesus in cultures throughout the world Church. It will necessarily be very summary but should give a good idea of the range of thinking about Jesus today. A number of anthologies have been produced where one can find more about the emerging images of Jesus in our time.[1]

I. Images in Africa

African theologians have been a particularly fertile source of images of Jesus as a way of relating Jesus more closely to African cultures. In doing so, their concern has been not only to be more faithful to the humanity of Jesus but also to find correlates in the Bible and subsequent Christian tradition. Four such images are of special note: Christ as ancestor, as master of initiation, as healer, as abundant life.

Christ as Ancestor.[2] Perhaps the most striking image of Jesus for non-Africans has been that of Christ as ancestor. Much of sub-Saharan Africa, like East and South Asia, has a highly developed system of veneration of ancestors. Ancestors are seen as guardians of the morality of the living as well as intermediaries with God on their behalf. In many places, there is a strong sense of the all-pervading presence of the ancestors.

Even though Christ is not in the blood lineage of African peoples, he has been adopted into those lineages as their spiritual progenitor. Even though he had no physical offspring and died a violent death at a young age (all qualities that would ordinarily disqualify one from becoming an ancestor), he is seen as having given his life on the cross to save us (young warriors killed defending the people could qualify as ancestors) that all might have life. Paul's discourse on Jesus as the New Adam in Romans 5 is seen as the biblical anchor for this image. Jesus, as our spiritual Proto-Ancestor, intercedes for us before the throne of God.

Jesus as Ancestor has been a controversial image in Africa, and by no means universally accepted. In some cultures, ancestors are not considered benevolent protectors of their descendants, but rather quarrelsome figures. The image has been perhaps more important to theologians than to ordinary Christians. Nonetheless, it remains an important, mediating image.

Christ as Master of Initiation.[3] Roughly half the world's cultures have rites of initiation whereby children pass to adulthood. In Francophone Africa, an image of Jesus that has arisen is that of Master of Initiation. In this role, Christ leads us, by his death and resurrection, to our transformation and salvation. This becomes a way of explaining the meaning of the suffering, death, and resurrection of Christ. Just as no one can become a master of the initiation rites without having first passed through them him- or herself, so too Christ had to die in order that we might live in communion with God.

Christ the Healer. Healing and healers play a central role in most African cultures, as they do in other small-scale societies around the world. The fact that Jesus has so often been portrayed in the Gospels as a healer made this a natural choice of image for Africans. Only recently has this image been re-appropriated in the secular West (Enlightenment thinking having discounted the possibility of healing); one would like to think that African theology has contributed to this renewed appreciation of this image.

Christ as Abundant Life. Diane Stinton has engaged in empirical research in a number of Anglophone countries in Africa as to images of Jesus – among theologians, pastors, and ordinary people.[4] The one she has found most commonly was that of Jesus as Life-Giver or Abundant Life. The story of Jesus at the well with the Samaritan woman in John 4:1–42 is often pointed to as a bible source of this image. Fullness of life is at the heart of what many African peoples see as the goal of being human. This, then, becomes a natural image to seize upon.

II. Jesus in Asia

Asia has the lowest percentage of Christians of any continent. Two images of Jesus stand out especially here: Jesus as teacher or sage; and Jesus among poor, marginalized groups.

Jesus the Sage. The great figures associated with religions in Asia are teachers or sages. One thinks of the Buddha, the gurus of India, or of Confucius in this regard. It is not surprising, then, that this would form a natural source of imagery for Jesus. Since Jesus is so often portrayed as a teacher in the Gospels, and as the source of divine wisdom (especially in the Gospel of John), the biblical foundation for seeing Jesus as Sage is quite obvious and clear.[5]

Jesus among the Poor. The Federation of Asian Bishops' Conferences has said that there need to be three dialogues in Asia if Christianity is to take root there: the dialogue of religions, the dialogue of cultures, and the dialogue with the poor. In a number of countries, this theme has been taken up explicitly.[6] In India, it has been especially with the *dalits*, those Indians at the very bottom of society. Today, the majority of Christianity in India come from among the *dalits*. Jesus as *dalit* shows his profound identification with the poorest and most despised of the poor.

The other major area where Jesus' identification with the marginalized has been explored was in the *minjung* theologies in Korea in the 1980s. *Minjung* means the ordinary people. Especially during the struggles of people – especially workers and students – in South Korea to overcome the military dictatorships of the 1970s and early 1980s Jesus as *minjung* had a special salience.[7]

III. Jesus in Latin America

Images of Jesus dating from the colonial era remain vibrant among Latin Americans today (as they do in the Philippines, which were evangelized from Mexico). Images of the infant Jesus (*el Santo Niño* or *el Niño Dios*) and of the suffering Christ in his passion (as well as the dead Christ) can be found throughout Latin America. Although brought by the Spaniards to Latin America, they have also taken on additional meaning, blending indigenous ideas and traditions with the Christian message.

The rise of the liberation theologies in Latin America contributed to a host of images of Jesus as Liberator, the Jesus of the Poor, and Jesus the Non-Person (either as a person of no significance or, during the years of military rule, the person who had been 'disappeared' or abducted). Although theologies of liberation are less in evidence today than in the 1970s and 1980s, these images of the poor Jesus are still very much present in Latin American cultures today.[8]

Finally, one should note the rise of theologies among indigenous peoples in Latin America. They have images of Jesus that sometimes meld with older, indigenous traditions, or represent variations on the liberation themes that are found in Latin America.[9]

IV. Jesus in the North Atlantic

Jesus as a member of Black, Hispanic, and indigenous cultures – as someone identifying with them and espousing their cause – can be found in North America.[10] For the Caucasian population of North America and Europe, however, one has not seen the same kind of systematic work as has come from the contextual theologies elsewhere.[11] A more informal picture can be sketched, however.

Since 1975, I have been teaching an introductory course in Christology and Cultures at the graduate level. Each year, by means of an exercise to elicit from the students their own images of Jesus, I have been able to draw up a profile of Caucasian students. In the 1970s, students typically had more divine images of Jesus than human ones; since that time into the present, that balance has exactly reversed. Images prominent for students since the mid-1980s have been Jesus as friend, as brother, as teacher, and as healer. This represents the shift to more horizontal, human images than from an earlier period (when Jesus as Son of God, as judge, and as Lord prevailed). They see Jesus (in their own description) as someone who understands them, befriends them, and does not judge them. He is a Jesus who heals their wounds. Since the early 1990s, Jesus as one who befriends women is also quite salient (for men as well as for women). While graduate students in theology are hardly representative of the general Christian population, it does give some indication of how Jesus may be seen in an affluent, secularizing, and pluralist society. Use of the same instrument among other groups has turned up largely the same images.

Conclusion

In the images of Jesus that have come to the fore across the world Church, one finds them clustering in two places. On the one hand, Jesus is placed at the centre of the culture. He is a member of the culture and utterly identifies with it. He is supremely human, yet can also (in many of the images) mediate the divine as well. The divinity is less apparent in Caucasian North Atlantic groups, where secularization has made the greatest cultural inroads.

On the other hand, Jesus is at the margins of a culture, identifying with those who are excluded or marginalized. Again, there is a sense of profound identification. While that is evident in this solidarity with the marginalized and the poor, that Jesus has to be more than just human; he has to be a source of ultimate liberation and inclusion for them. In these two juxtapositions, then, we can see how the divine and the human Jesus are being mediated among Christians today.

Notes

1. Some examples are José Miguez Bonino (ed.), *Faces of Jesus: Latin American Christologies*, Maryknoll, NY: Orbis Books, 1984; Anton Wessels, *Images of Jesus: How Jesus is Perceived and Portrayed in Non-Western Cultures*, Grand Rapids: Eerdmans, 1990; Robert Schreiter (ed.), *Faces of Jesus in Africa*, Maryknoll, NY: Orbis Books, 1992; R. S. Surgirtharajah (ed.), *Asian Faces of*

Jesus, Maryknoll, NY: Orbis Books, 1993; Manuel Marzal (ed.), *The Indian Face of God in Latin America*, Maryknoll, NY: Orbis Books, 1996; Doris Strahm, *Von Rand in die Mitte: Christologie aus der Sicht von Frauen in Asien, Afrika, und Lateinamerika*, Luzern: Ed. Exodus, 1997; Volker Kuester, *The Many Faces of Jesus Christ: Intercultural Christology*, Maryknoll, NY: Orbis Books, 2001.

2. The most comprehensive account is in Charles Nyamiti, *Christ Our Ancestor*, Gweru: Mambo Press, 1984.

3. See especially Anselme Titianma Sanon, *Das Evangelium verwurzeln. Glaubenserschliessung im Raum afrikanischer Stammesinitiationen*, Freiburg: Herder, 1985.

4. Diane Stinton, *Jesus of Africa*, Maryknoll, NY: Orbis Books, 2004.

5. For one rendering of this see Thomas Thangaraj, *The Crucified Guru*, Nashville: Abingdon Press, 1994.

6. For an overview of these christologies, see Kuester, *op. cit.*

7. See David Kwang-sun Suh, *The Minjung in Christ*, Singapore: The Christian Conference of Asia, 1991.

8. See Miguez Bonino, *op. cit.*

9. Less has been written in this area, but they are in evidence in the five congresses for indigenous theology that have been held throughout Latin America. See also Marzal, *op. cit.*

10. Albert Cleage, *The Black Messiah*, New York: Sheed and Ward, 1968; Virgilio Elizondo, *Galilean Journey*, Maryknoll, NY: Orbis Books, 2000; Achiel Peelman, *Christ is a Native American*, Ottawa: Novalis, 2006.

11. One more cultural than theological work is Stephen Prothero, *American Jesus*, New York: Farrar, Straus and Giroux, 2003.

An Annotated Basic Bibliography on the Historical Jesus

BARBAGLIO, G. *Gesù ebreo di Galilea. Indagine storica*. Bologna: Dehoniane, 2003.

The book gathers what the author considers most noteworthy and apposite in contemporary scholarship. Perhaps its major contribution lies in the large number of texts assembled to aid contextualization of Jesus' message and actions (Qumran, Flavius Josephus, Philo, Mishna . . .).

CROSSAN, J. D. *The Historical Jesus. The Life of a Mediterranean Jewish Peasant*. San Franciso, CA: Harper, 1991.

Crossan is undoubtedly the most popular and also the most daring of US students of the person of Jesus. His fascinating reconstruction of Jesus' actions has made his books into real bestsellers. Nevertheless, there is considerable dispute over his position on sources (Gospel of Thomas, Gospel of Peter . . .), his reconstruction of the figure of Jesus as a Jewish cynic, his analysis of the passion narratives, and his view of the birth of the Easter faith. His strength lies in his brilliant observations on Jesus' table-fellowship, his healing and exorcising activity, the relationship between his itinerant followers and sedentary disciples, and his socio-political dimension.

DUNN, J. D. G. *Jesus Remembered*. Grand Rapids, MI and Cambridge: Eerdmans, 2003.
———. *A New Perspective on Jesus. What the Quest for the Historical Jesus Missed*. Grand Rapids, MI: Baker Publishing Group, 2005.

Dunn has recently criticized two aspects of modern research into the historical Jesus: (1) the obsession with reaching a 'pure Jesus' by eliminating everything supposedly added in Christian tradition, without appreciating the 'impact' Jesus made on his closest followers; (2) the lack of attention paid to 'oral transmission' and ignorance of its most characteristic working and features. Evidence suggests that Dunn's criticism is being well received in certain quarters.

FREYNE, S. *Galilee and Gospel.* Boston-Leiden: Brill, 2002.
————. *Jesus, a Jewish Galilean.* London & New York: T. & T. Clark International, 2005.

After a lifetime totally dedicated to the study of the Galilee of Jesus, Freyne is now an authority on reconstructing the socio-cultural context in which Jesus lived and acted. His numerous excellent studies shed new and profound light on the sayings and actions of the Prophet from Galilee.

HORSLEY, R. A. *Galilee: History, Politics, People.*, Harrisburg, PA: Trinity Press International, 1995.
————. *Archaeology, History and Society in Galilee. The Social Context of Jesus and the Rabbis.* Harrisburg, PA: Trinity Press International, 1996.
————. *Sociology and the Jesus Movement.* New York: Continuum, 1994.

Starting from the socio-political context of first-century Palestine (rather than from textual criticism), the author, one of the most popular US scholars, reconstructs the figure of Jesus as a revolutionary leader of a peaceful bent who sought to lay the bases for a new social order in Galilee.

GNILKA, J. *Jesus von Nazaret. Botschaft und Geschichte.* Freiburg im Breisgau: Herder, 1990.

In the German-speaking world this work marks the passage from research into Jesus based on critical study of the literary sources to the utilization of all types of disciplines and of historico-critical methods of familiarizing ourselves with the political, religious, and social context that can shed light on his person. This balanced and well-researched study has become a standard work of reference in Europe.

MEIER, J. P. *A Marginal Jesus.* New York: Bantam, Doubleday, Dell, 1991–.

A monumental work (still unfinished) providing a virtually exhaustive study of the major questions concerning Jesus. It is considered the most objective and best-reasoned reconstruction in the field of Catholic research. Its full and rigorous treatment of the subjects makes this an indispensable tool for research into Jesus.

SANDERS, E. P. *Jesus and Judaism.* London: SCM Press, 1985.

The author is one of the greatest modern specialists on ancient Judaism and the origins of Christianity. He presents a Jesus very much part of the Jewish world of his time. In this work he studies primarily Jesus' relationships with his contemporaries and the causes of his death. An indispensable writer for study of the Jewish character of Jesus today.

————. *The Historical Figure of Jesus.* London: SCM Press, 1993.

This work by the great U.S. scholar is a more summary and popular book. It brings together the conclusions the author has reached after long years of research into the Jewish context in which Jesus lived. He tackles all the subjects with great mastery, bringing out, as he habitually does, the Jewish nature of Jesus.

SCHLOSSER, J. *Jésus de Nazareth.* Paris: Agnes Vienot Éditions,1999.

The author, who lectures in the Catholic Theology Faculty at Strasbourg University, is one of the best known European specialists on Jesus and the New Testament. This work is written with the intention of drawing together the most accepted conclusions on the most fundamental aspects of Jesus' message and actions. His reasoning processes, his critical analyses, and his study of the context of the time are all clearly set out.

THEISSEN, G. and A. MERZ. *Der historische Jesus. Ein Lehrbuch.* Göttingen: Vandenhoeck & Ruprecht, 1996. *The Historical Jesus.* London: SCM Press, 1998.

The best and most complete manual of the results of historical research on

Jesus. It tackles all the essential questions in an ordered and well-founded manner. The work is, to a large extent, the fruit of many years of research by Theissen, the most respected European specialist in study of the historical Jesus and in particular of the 'Jesus movement'. The work is presented as a text book, with numerous diagrams and tables.

Compiled by J. A. Pagola
Translated by Paul Burns

Contributors

ERIK BORGMAN, born in Amsterdam in 1957, is Professor for Systematic Theology – Theology of Religion, especially Christianity – in the Department of Religious Studies and Theology of Tilburg University, The Netherlands. He is married with two daughters and is a Lay Dominican. He studied philosophy and theology at the University of Nijmegen and wrote a dissertation on the different forms of liberation theology and their relation to academic Western theology (promotion 1990). Between 1998 and 2004 he worked for the Dutch Province of the Order of Preachers to study and keep alive the theology of Edward Schillebeeckx. He has published *Edward Schillebeeckx: a Theologian in his History*, Vol. I: *A Catholic Theology of Culture* (2003). Between 2000 and 2007 he worked at the interdisciplinary Heyendaal Institute for theology, sciences, and culture at Radboud University, Nijmegen, from 2004 as its academic director. A member of the Board of Directors and the Presidential Board of *Concilium*, he has written extensively on the relation between theology, religion, the Christian tradition and contemporary culture.

Address: Department of Religious Studies and Theology, Office D 146, PO Box 90153, NL - 5000 LE Tilburg
E-mail: E.Borgman@hin.ru.nl; Borgman-VanLeusden@hetnet.nl

LISA SOWLE CAHILL is the J. Donald Monan Professor of Theology at Boston College, Newton Massachusetts, USA. She is the author of *Theological Bioethics: Participation, Justice and Change*; and *Sex, Gender and Christian Ethics*. She is a past president of the Catholic Theological Society of America and of the Society of Christian Ethics (North America).

Address: 21 Campanella Way, Room 321, Boston College, Chestnut Hill, MA 02467, USA
E-mail: Lisa.Cahill@bc.edu; cahilll@mail.bc.edu

SEAN FREYNE is former Professor of Theology at Trinity College, Dublin, and is currently Visiting Professor of Early Christian History and Literature, Harvard Divinity School, Cambridge, USA. He is a former member of the editorial board of *Concilium* and a past-President of the Society for the Study of the New Testament. He is a frequent contributor to discussion programmes on radio and television. Among his more recent publications are *Galilee and Gospel. Selected Essays* (2000), *Texts, Contexts and Cultures. Essays on Biblical Topics* (2002), and *Jesus, a Jewish Galilean. A New Reading of the Jesus Story* (2004).

Address: Harvard Divinity School, 45 Francis Avenue, Cambridge/MA 02138, USA
E-mail: sfreyne@tcd.ie

KARL GABRIEL was born in 1943. He studied Catholic theology and sociology and passed the examinations for first degrees at Tübingen University (1969) and Bielefeld University (1973). He was awarded a doctorate for his dissertation in sociology at Bielefeld (1977) and presented his thesis for qualification as a lecturer in theology at Würzburg (1992). He was a research assistant at Bielefeld (1974-80). He was appointed to a chair in sociology, pastoral sociology, and aid studies at the North German Catholic University at Osnabrück-Vechta; which he held from 1980 to 1998. Since 1998 he has been professor in Christian social studies in the Catholic theological faculty of the Westphalian Wilhelms-University of Münster and director of the Institute of Christian Social Sciences He has published several books and articles on the sociology of religion and ecclesiastical sociology, research in the field of welfare organizations, and Christian social ethics.

Address: Westfälische Wilhelms- Universität Münster, Institut Für Christliche Sozialwissenschaften, Hüfferstr, 27, D-48149, Münster, Germany
E-mail: gabrielk@uni-muenster.de

ROSINO GIBELLINI holds doctorates in theology from the Gregorian University in Roma and in philosophy from the Catholic University of Milan. He is literary director of Editrice Queriniana in Brescia, for which he has founded and directs the collections 'Giornale di teologia (from 1966) and 'Biblioteca di teologia contemporanea' (from 1969), with the purpose of opening Italian theology and culture to international theological thought.

He is the author of studies of Teilhard de Chardin, Moltmann, and Pannenberg. His most recent publications include *La teologia del XX secolo* (1992; sixth, enlarged ed. 2007); and he has edited the collective volumes *Dio nella filosofia del Novecento* (1993, ²2004) and *Prospettive teologiche per il XXI secolo* (2003, ²2006).

Address: Editrice Queriniana, Via Ferri, Nr. 75, I-25.123 Brescia (BS), Italy
E-mail: direzione@queriniana.it; Rosino@numerica.it

JOSÉ IGNACIO GONÁLEZ FAUS was born 1933 in Valencia (Spain) and is a Jesuit priest. He is professor emeritus of systematic theology in the faculty of Barcelona and at the UCA in El Salvador). From 1981 to 2006 he was academic director of the 'Cristianismo y Justicia' Centre in Barcelona. His publications include *La Humanidad Nueva. Ensayo de Cristología* (⁹2000); *Proyecto de hermano. Visión creyente del hombre* (³2000); *Vicarios de Cristo. Los pobres en la teología y espiritualidad cristianas* (³2006); *Ningún obispo impuesto. Las elecciones episcopales en la historia de la Iglesia* (1992); *La autoridad de la verdad. Momentos oscuros del magisterio eclesiástico* (²2006). His most recent work is *El rostro humano de Dios. De la revolución de Jesús a la divinidad de Jesús* (²2008).

Address: Centre Borja, Llaceres 30, E-08190 Sant Cugat del Vallès, Barcelona, Spain
E-mail: gfaus@fespinal.com

ROGER HAIGHT, S.J., teaches theology at Union Theological Seminary in New York. He is the author of *Jesus Symbol of God* (1999) and a three-volume historical and systematic work on the Church entitled *Christian Community in History* (2004–2008). He is a past president of the Catholic Theological Society of America and the Divinity School of the University of Chicago's Alumnus of the Year of 2005.

Address: 3041 Broadway, BT 409, New York/NY 10027, USA
E-mail: rhaight@wjst.edu; rdhaight@aol.com

HANSPETER HEINZ is Professor Emeritus in pastoral theology at Augsburg University and chairs the 'Jews and Christians' discussion group of the Central Committee of German Catholics. Together with fifteen other

Jewish and Christian authors, he also contributed to a book edited by Rabbi Walter Homolka and Professor Erich Zenger: '. . . *damit sie Jesus Christus erkennen' – die neue Karfreitagsfürbitte in der Diskussion* (2008).

Address: Gögginger Mauer 19, 86150 Augsburg, Germany.
E-mail: hanspeter.heinz@t-online.de.

MARIA CLARA LUCCHETTI BINGEMER is a lecturer and researcher in the theology department of the Pontifical Catholic University of Rio de Janeiro (PUC-RJ). She gained a doctorate in systematic theology from the Gregorian in Rome, with a thesis on Trinitarian mysticism and Christian praxis in St Ignatius of Loyola. She is currently dean of the theology centre and the human sciences faculty of the PUC-RJ. For ten years she directed the Centro Loyola de Fé e Cultura, which aims to offer lay people in particular an integral (human, spiritual, doctrinal and ethical) formation by means of dialogue between faith, culture, and other religious traditions. Her most recent works are *Deus Trindade, a Vida no Coração do Mundo* (with Vitor Feller, 2008); *A argila e o espírito* (articles and essays; 2004); *Um rosto para Deus?* (2005); *Simone Weil - A força e a fraqueza do amor* (2007).

Address: Pontifícia Universidade Católica do Rio de Janeiro, Depto. de Teologia (TEO), Rua Marquês de São Vicente, 225, Edifício Cardeal Leme 11 andar, Caixa Postal: 38097, 22453-900 - Rio de Janeiro - RJ – Brasil
E-mail : agape@rdc.puc-rio.br

SILVIA SCATENA was born in 1970 and graduated from Pisa University. She received a PhD in Contemporary History from the University of Rome 3 and has been Visiting Fellow for a semester at the School of Religious Studies of the Catholic University in Washington D.C. She is a long-term participant in the work of the Foundation for Religious Sciences of Bologna and teaches Contemporary History at the universities of Modena and Reggio Emilia. Her main writings are: *La fatica della libertà. L'elaborazione della dichiarazione 'Dignitatis humanae' sulla libertà religiosa del Vaticano II* (2003), and *In populo pauperum. La chiesa latinoamericana dal concilio a Medellín (1962-1968)* (2007).

Address: San Vitale 114, 40125 Bologna, Italy
E-mail: silviascat@virgilio.it; scatena.silvia@unimore.it

ROBERT SCHREITER, born in 1947, is professor of theology at the Catholic Theological Union in Chicago (USA). He has worked extensively in contextual theology, in globalization, in social reconciliation, and in the mission of the Church. He edits the Faith and Culture Series for Orbis Books and is an editor of the journal *Studies in Interreligious Dialogue*, among others. His books include *Constructing Local Theologies* (1985), *The New Catholicity: Theology between the Global and Local* (1997), *Reconciliation: Mission and Ministry in a Changing Social Order* (1992), and *The Minisry of Reconciliation: Spirituality and Strategies* (1998).

Address: Catholic Theological Union, 5401 South Cornell Ave., Chicago/ IL 60615-5698, USA
E-mail: rschreit@ctu.edu,

JON SOBRINO was born in Barcelona to Basque parents in 1938 and educated in Spain, Germany, and the USA, from whcre he holds a Master's Degree in Engineering. He joined the Society of Jesus in 1956 and has since 1957 belonged to the Central American Province and lived mainly in El Salvador. He is professor of theology and director of the Mgr Romero Centre at the Catholic University of Central America in San Salvador. He is joint editor with Ignacio Ellacuria, the Rector of the university, murdered in 1993, of *Mysterium Liberationsis: Fundamental Concepts of Liberation Theology* (1991; Eng. ed. 1993). Among his more recent publications translated into English are the two-volume christology *Jesus the Liberator* (1993) and *Christ the Liberator* (2001); *Cartas a Ellacuría* (2004); *Fuera de los pobres no hay salvación, Pequeños ensayos utóico-proféticos* (2007).

Address: Universidad Centroamericana, Centro Monseñor Romero, Apartado (01) 168, San Salvador (El Salvador), C. A.
E-mail: jsobrino@cmr.uca.edu.sv

ANDRÉS TORRES QUEIRUGA was born in 1940 and holds doctorates in philosophy from the University of Santiago de Compostela and in theology from the Gregorian in Rome. He taught fundamental theology at the Theological Institute in Santiago from 1968 to 1987 and is currently professor of philosophy of religion at the university there. He is editor of *Encrucillada: Revista Galega de Pensamento Cristián*, as well as being on the editorial board of *Iglesia Viva*, an advisor to *Revista Portuguesa de Filosofia*, and a founding

member of the Spanish Society for Sciences of Religion. His many published works include *Recuperar la salvación* (1977; ³2001); *Creo en Dios Padre*
(⁵1998), *Recuperar la creación* (1997; trans. into Portugese and German); *Fin
del cristianismo premoderno* (2000), *Repensar la resurrección* (2003), *Esperanza
a pesar del mal* (2005); *Repensar la revelación: La revelación divina en la
realización humana* (2008; revised ed. of 1977, trans. into Italian, Portuguese,
and German).

Address: O. Courraliña 23 G, 15705 Santiago de Compostela, La Coruña,
Spain
E-mail: atorres@usc.es; torresqueiruga@gmail.com

FELIX WILFRED was born in Tamil Nadu, India, in 1948. He is the President
of the faculty of arts, and Chairman of the School of Philosophy and
Religious Thought, State University of Madras. He is also a member of the
Statutory Ethical Committee of Indian Institute of Technology, Madras. He
has been a member of the International Theological Commission of the
Vatican. As visiting professor, he has taught at the Universities of Nijmegen,
Münster, Frankfurt am Main, Boston College, and Ateneo de Manila. His
researches and field studies today cut across many disciplines in humanities
and social sciences. His more recent publications in the field of theology are
On the Banks of Ganges (²2002), *Asian Dreams and Christian Hope* (²2003),
The Sling of Utopia: Struggles for a Different Society (2005), and *Margins:
Site of Asian Theologies* (2008). He was elected president of the board of
Concilium in 2007.

Address: University of Madras, Dept. of Christian Studies, Chepauk,
Madras 600 005, India
E-mail: fwilfred@satyam.net.in

Concilium Subscription Information

February   2009/1: *Heritage*

April   2009/2: *Theology of Creation*

June   2009/3: *God, Monotheism*

October   2009/4: *Fathers of Latin American Theology*

December   2009/5: *Translation of the Bible*

New subscribers: to receive *Concilium 2008* (five issues) anywhere in the world, please copy this form, complete it in block capitals and send it with your payment to the address below.

Please enter my subscription for *Concilium 2008*

Individuals	Institutions
____ £40.00 UK	____ £55.00 UK
____ £60.00 overseas	____ £75.00 overseas
____ $110.00 North America/Rest of World	____ $140 North America/Rest of World
____ €99.00 Europe	____ €125.00 Europe

Postage included – airmail for overseas subscribers

Payment Details:
Payment must accompany all orders and can be made by cheque or credit card
I enclose a cheque for £/$/€ _____ Payable to SCM-Canterbury Press Ltd
Please charge my Visa/MasterCard (Delete as appropriate) for £/$/€ _____
Credit card number ....
Expiry date ....
Signature of cardholder ....
Name on card ....
Telephone .... E-mail ....

Send your order to *Concilium*, SCM-Canterbury Press Ltd
13–17 Long Lane, London EC1A 9PN, UK
E-Mail: office@scm-canterburypress.co.uk

Customer service information:
All orders must be prepaid. Subscriptions are entered on an annual basis (i.e. January to December). No refunds on subscriptions will be made after the first issue of the Journal has been despatched. If you have any queries or require information about other payment methods, please contact our Customer Services department.